Luke

INTERPRETATION
BIBLE STUDIES

Interpretation Bible Studies
from Westminster John Knox Press

Genesis
Celia Brewer Marshall

Exodus
James D. Newsome

First and Second Samuel
David Hester

Psalms
Jerome F. D. Creach

Isaiah
Gary W. Light

Jeremiah
Robert R. Laha Jr.

Matthew
Alyce M. McKenzie

Mark
Richard I. Deibert

Luke
Thomas W. Walker

John
Mark A. Matson

Acts
Charles C. Williamson

Romans
Art Ross and Martha M. Stevenson

First Corinthians
Bruce N. Fisk

Philippians and Galatians
Stanley P. Saunders

Revelation
William C. Pender

Luke

THOMAS W. WALKER

Westminster John Knox Press
LOUISVILLE • LONDON

For my parents, Andy and Frances,
who instilled a love of scripture within me,
and for Jan, Worth, and Chris,
who share that love with me today

© 2001 Thomas W. Walker
Leader's Guide © 1998 Westminster John Knox Press

The photographs on pages 10, 18, 49, 60, 71, 78, 85, and 98 are © SuperStock, Inc. The photograph on page 30 is © PhotoDisc, Inc.

Book design by Drew Stevens
Cover design by Pam Poll
Cover illustration by Robert Stratton

First edition
Published by Westminster John Knox Press
Louisville, Kentucky

This book is printed on acid-free paper that meets the American National Standards Institute Z39.48 standard. ♾

PRINTED IN THE UNITED STATES OF AMERICA

01 02 03 04 05 06 07 08 09 10 — 10 9 8 7 6 5 4 3 2 1

Library of Congress Cataloging-in-Publication Data

A catalog record for this book is available from the Library of Congress.

ISBN 0-664-22691-4

Contents

Series Introduction

The Bible has long been revered for its witness to God's presence and redeeming activity in the world; its message of creation and judgment, love and forgiveness, grace and hope; its memorable characters and stories; its challenges to human life; and its power to shape faith. For generations people have found in the Bible inspiration and instruction, and, for nearly as long, commentators and scholars have assisted students of the Bible. This series, Interpretation Bible Studies (IBS), continues that great heritage of scholarship with a fresh approach to biblical study.

Designed for ease and flexibility of use for either personal or group study, IBS helps readers not only to learn about the history and theology of the Bible, understand the sometimes difficult language of biblical passages, and marvel at the biblical accounts of God's activity in human life, but also to accept the challenge of the Bible's call to discipleship. IBS offers sound guidance for deepening one's knowledge of the Bible and for faithful Christian living in today's world.

IBS was developed out of three primary convictions. First, the Bible is the church's scripture and stands in a unique place of authority in Christian understanding. Second, good scholarship helps readers understand the truths of the Bible and sharpens their perception of God speaking through the Bible. Third, deep knowledge of the Bible bears fruit in one's ethical and spiritual life.

Each IBS volume has ten brief units of key passages from a book of the Bible. By moving through these units, readers capture the sweep of the whole biblical book. Each unit includes study helps, such as maps, photos, definitions of key terms, questions for reflection, and suggestions for resources for further study. In the back of each volume is a Leader's Guide that offers helpful suggestions on how to use IBS.

The Interpretation Bible Studies series grows out of the well-known Interpretation commentaries (John Knox Press), a series that helps preachers and teachers in their preparation. Although each IBS volume bears a deep kinship to its companion Interpretation commentary, IBS can stand alone. The reader need not be familiar with the Interpretation commentary to benefit from IBS. However, those who want to discover even more about the Bible will benefit by consulting Interpretation commentaries too.

Through the kind of encounter with the Bible encouraged by the Interpretation Bible Studies, the church will continue to discover God speaking afresh in the scriptures.

Introduction to Luke

> Since many have undertaken to set down an orderly account of the events that have been fulfilled among us, just as they were handed on to us by those who from the beginning were eyewitnesses and servants of the word, I too decided, after investigating everything carefully from the very first, to write an orderly account for you, most excellent Theophilus, so that you may know the truth concerning the things about which you have been instructed.
>
> —Luke 1:1–4

Something has happened. In a world in which people search for meaning, in a time when chaos and disorder call into question order and structure, something has happened. The Gospel of Luke opens with these words of introduction that boldly claim that something has happened, something that has significance for the entire world. Unlike the other three Gospels, Luke's Gospel begins with a direct address to the reader that sets the stage for what follows in the retelling of the story of Jesus. Something has happened that offers "truth" and sense to the complexity of the world, order in the midst of chaos, hope in the midst of darkness, and a narrative in the midst of a cacophony of competing claims. We spend much of our lives trying to make "sense" of the moments that weave themselves in and out of our daily existence. We find ourselves seeking order, wondering about connections to the past, trying to understand the present, and seeking guidance for the future. Many voices offer us constructs with which to imagine our lives. From the lifestyles of the rich and famous to the fire and brimstone of the street preacher, narratives are offered to us that guide, instruct, cajole, and shape our lives as we search for meaning.

Luke's Gospel sets out to make sense of the world for those who read it. It offers a narrative, "*the* narrative," through which all other life stories are to be read. It offers truth for those seeking it, order for those facing disorder, and purpose for those who think that the world makes no sense. In the first four verses of this telling of his good news, Luke informs his readers that what they are about to read is *the* history through which all other histories must be understood.

Author and Situation

The third Gospel offers few clues to the identity of its author. Any attempt to gain insight into the author of this Gospel is tied also to understanding the author's sequel, the Acts of the Apostles. Tradition has ascribed this Gospel and Acts to Luke, the physician and the companion of Paul (Col. 4:14; 2 Tim. 4:11; Philemon 24). Both the Gospel and Acts begin with an introduction that addresses a certain "Theophilus" but does not provide the name of the author, so that these works remain anonymous (for convenience we will continue to refer to the author as Luke).

While not providing the author's name, the introduction of the Gospel does shed light on Luke's context. The author is a member of the Christian community, as he refers to events that have been fulfilled among *us* and the traditions that have been passed down to *us*. The introduction mentions that Luke has gathered information for his narrative from eyewitnesses and other narratives; this is a key factor and it has led most scholars to place the composition of Luke in the latter part of the first century, sometime after 70 C.E. and probably before 90 C.E. An abundant use of the Greek version of the Old Testament, both in direct quotes and in allusions, and a superb use of literary techniques such as foreshadowing and suspense, suggest that the author of the third Gospel was a Hellenistic Christian with some education.

> **Who was Luke?**
> The author of Luke—who may or may not have been Luke, the physician and companion of Paul—was apparently a member of the Christian community. He may have been a Gentile Christian or a convert from Hellenistic Judaism. He probably did his writing not as an eyewitness to the events he writes about but as a second- or third-generation recipient of the tradition. For more detail, see Craddock, *Luke*, Interpretation, 16–17.

Although we do not learn the author's name, the Gospel does address a specific reader with the name Theophilus. Scholars have long debated whether this name referred to a specific, historic individual or was a general title referring to anyone who would follow Jesus as a "friend of God." In either case, the introduction suggests that this Theophilus is "informed" with the tradition, either having researched it or having received it through the instruction of the early Christian community. Through the mention of Theophilus, Luke's Gospel designates all those who have confronted the traditions and narratives regarding Jesus and are continuing to try and make sense of that narrative. In light of the historical situation of the late first century C.E., questions about the relation between the church and the synagogue, about the relations between the church and the Roman Empire, about the church's identity in the world, and about the significance of Jesus would be in the air for those acquainted with the story, and these, among others, would find themselves addressed in Luke's orderly account.

"An orderly account" (Luke 1:3)

With these words, Luke describes the material that will appear in the narrative that follows. Other accounts of the life of Christ have been written, but apparently questions remain, and Luke will now attempt to answer those questions. Central to Luke's approach is his understanding of God's activity and movement through history. From the glimpses of angels by Zechariah and Mary to the Emmaus road, Luke portrays the world as a place through which the living God is moving and moving with a purpose. The purposive movement of God through history can be clearly seen in the frequent use of the phrase "it is necessary," found uniquely in Luke's retelling of the life of Jesus (e.g., Luke 2:49; 4:43; 13:16; 13:33, etc.). For Luke, God is the central actor on the stage of the world.

The crux of God's movement, however, is Jesus, and it is his story that Luke tells in the third Gospel. As the crux of history, Jesus provides the focal point for understanding God's activity in the past and for understanding the future life of those who would follow him, the church. The world is not simply a random combination of atoms and history is not haphazard, but God has been moving through history purposefully and in Jesus those

> For further reading about the Gospel of Luke, see Fred B. Craddock, *Luke*, Interpretation (Louisville, Ky.: John Knox Press, 1990); Sharon H. Ringe, *Luke*, Westminster Bible Companion (Louisville, Ky.: Westminster John Knox Press, 1995); William Barclay, *The Gospel of Luke*, Daily Study Bible (Philadelphia: Westminster Press, 1975).

purposes shine clearly. So he is the interpretive clue to understanding the scriptures of the Old Testament and was anticipated by those scriptures; thus, Luke will constantly allude to those scriptures both directly and indirectly. Likewise, the life of Jesus sets the parameters for the life of the church that follows in his footsteps, a life of obedience and of suffering rejection by the world, so the narrative will spend time on understanding Jesus' identity and will include a sequel (Acts) concerning those who bear that identity.

Jesus is the center point of God's movement in history and also the clearest revelation of God's purposes. From the beginning, Luke reports that the key to understanding Jesus is engaging him as "savior" (Luke 2:11) of the world. For Luke, Jesus is the embodied presence of the grace, mercy, and saving purposes of God. Yet Luke appears to realize that his readers have expectations and presuppositions about salvation and what it means that Jesus is savior. Throughout his presentation, Luke invites the followers of Jesus to have their concept of salvation critiqued and overturned. Meeting this Jesus and understanding salvation through him is not a simple acquiescence but a response to a radical call to believe and see the world differently—a vision that often turns the world upside down as the poor become rich, a vision that challenges cherished opinions about whom to treat as neighbor, and a vision that explodes the limits of grace.

Perhaps the deepest of all human longings is to make sense of our progression through history—through the ups and the downs, the joys and the sorrows. Luke provides a narrative to the "friend of God" in order that this friend might know the truth about God, and in knowing the truth begin to make sense of God's world. This truth spans the course of history and reaches forward into the unknown future. It is a truth that lays deep claims on the lives of those who would accept it, as Luke knows that these demands provide salvation and life abundant. In the midst of those who claim the world makes

Want to Know More?

About leading Bible study groups? See Roberta Hestenes, *Using the Bible in Groups* (Philadelphia: Westminster Press, 1983).

About the development of the Gospels? See William M. Ramsay, *The Westminster Guide to the Books of the Bible* (Louisville, Ky.: Westminster John Knox Press, 1994), 289–316; John Barton, *How the Bible Came to Be* (Louisville, Ky.: Westminster John Knox Press, 1997), 18–22, 44–46; Archibald M. Hunter, *Introducing the New Testament*, 3d rev. ed. (Philadelphia: Westminster Press, 1972), 23–26.

About the content or themes of each Gospel? See Duncan S. Ferguson, *Bible Basics: Mastering the Content of the Bible* (Louisville, Ky.: Westminster John Knox Press, 1995), 57–65; Hunter, *Introducing the New Testament*, 37–70.

no sense and those who offer other narratives, Luke offers the narrative of Jesus Christ as reassurance, challenge, promise, and hope. For Luke, this is the only narrative that makes sense of the past, offers guidance for the present, and secures hope for the future.

1 Luke 1:39–56

The Announcement of the Birth of Jesus

Birth announcements are a part of modern life. Parents, delighted over the arrival of newness in their lives, celebrate by sending hand-picked proclamations to family and friends. These proclamations contain vital information about the newborn such as date of birth, height, weight, and, of course, name. For most, the name claims the powerful present that exists in the newborn, but a name also connects the newborn to the past, to the history of his or her particular family. While these declarations of birth bear witness to the name of the child, they also speak about hopes and dreams that have been centered on the arrival of a child—dreams that have been fulfilled and hopes aroused that reach out into the uncertainty of the future.

Much like modern birth announcements, the narratives with which Luke begins his Gospel represent the culmination of promises that Luke finds in the Old Testament and the introduction of hopes for the future of God's interaction with God's people. In the birth stories related in Luke 1–2, we encounter Luke's unique perspective on the interconnectedness of history. For Luke, the old familiar hymn rings true: "God is working his purposes out." God had been at work in ancient Israel through Abraham and Sarah, David, and the prophets. God will be at work in the life, ministry, and mission of the child who will bear the name Jesus—that is, "God saves." Finally, God will continue to be at work through the church that arises after Jesus' death as the narratives in Luke's companion story, Acts, reveal. The birth stories firmly place the newborn child Jesus into God's history, so that Jesus is the fulfill-

> "Blessed are you among women, and blessed is the fruit of your womb."—Luke 1:42

6

ment of past promises and the hook upon which future hopes are hung. As Howard Marshall states, these stories are to be seen "not so much as a prelude to what follows but as the theme which is to be elaborated in the ensuing 'symphony of salvation'" (Marshall, 97).

Connecting to the Past and Setting the Stage

Luke's Gospel is steeped in the narratives and poetry of the Old Testament. Through both direct and indirect allusion, Luke ties the events of the life of Christ to the proclamations and hopes offered throughout the scriptures of the Hebrew people. These ties permeate the early chapters of Luke's Gospel, as he proclaims that God's continued plan and purpose for creation have become focused in the life and work of Jesus. Jesus' story begins like many stories of promise and newness in the Old Testament by focusing on barren women. Matthew begins his Gospel with a patrilineal genealogy (note well, however, the four "unique" women mentioned in Matthew's genealogy—Tamar, Rahab, Ruth, and the wife of Uriah, Bathsheba; see Matt. 1:1–18) and then a focus on Joseph. Luke, however, begins his telling with a focus on a barren couple, Zechariah and Elizabeth, and a woman, Mary, whose barrenness is not due to old age but to her unmarried status. These characters remain on center stage through the first two chapters of Luke's Gospel.

By focusing on Elizabeth and Mary, Luke picks up on a theme from the early narratives of promise in Genesis 12–50 and also from the narratives of 1 and 2 Samuel (see 1 Sam 1:1–2:10)—the theme of God's promise keeping in the face of incredible odds. Especially within the Genesis narratives, the apparent setting of the stories of father Abraham and mother Sarah is a world permeated by the promises of God, yet these promises are forever held in tension by the barren wombs of the ancient Israelite matriarchs. God promised

> ### The Stigma of Barrenness
>
> "In the absence of knowledge about the biological process of conception and the reasons for infertility, ancient cultures usually held the woman responsible for a couple's inability to conceive children. Her 'failure' was often interpreted as God's judgment against her, by which she brought suffering and shame on her husband."—Sharon H. Ringe, *Luke*, Westminster Bible Companion (Louisville, Ky.: Westminster John Knox Press, 1995), 28.

Abraham and Sarah that their descendants would be as numerous as the stars (Gen. 12:2; 15:5; 17:6), but Sarah was old and barren. The incongruity between the perceived reality of barrenness and the promise of future descendants finds its most poignant expression in the laughter of Abraham (Gen. 17:17) and Sarah (Gen. 18:12). As the story is told, the barrenness of Israel's matriarchs becomes symbolic for the void within creation that can only be filled through the promissory action of God.

Luke's description of Zechariah and Elizabeth carries the echo of the ancient Israelite stories. They receive a description that parallels that of Abraham and Sarah (Luke 1:7; compare Gen. 11:30) but can also be seen in the stories of Issac and Rebekah (Gen. 25:21), Jacob and Rachel (Gen. 29:31), Elkanah and Hannah (1 Sam. 1:5). Like Abraham and Sarah, Zechariah responds to the proclamation of a coming child with disbelief and incredulity and this leads to his muteness until the birth of John.

While this lack of faith resonates with the earlier narratives of Genesis, it also becomes a foil that highlights both the response of true faith and the difference between the promised children, John and Jesus. In a scene similar to Zechariah's visitation, Luke informs us that Gabriel made a second visit to a young girl named Mary. In both visits the same angelic announcer appears, bringing good news of a coming birth, news that includes the future activity and name of the soon-to-be-arriving child. Yet the reactions of the hearers of this news are vastly different. Whereas Zechariah responded in disbelief and was stricken mute, Mary responds in faith by hearing and obeying the word of God. Mary's response, "Here am I . . . ; let it be" (1:38), sets the stage for Luke's description of faith in God and the appropriate response to Jesus, the response of hearing and obeying (Luke 8:21; 11:27–28; see Tannehill, *Luke*, 53, and Brown, *Birth of the Messiah*). The distinction between the priest Zechariah's response of unbelief, a response by a representative of the religious establishment and one acquainted with the tradition, and Mary's response of obedience, a response by a woman and an outsider to the tradition, lays the groundwork for Luke's descriptions of the response of individuals throughout the Gospel. Jesus finds acceptance by the "outsiders" such

"Mary sings of the God who brings down the mighty and exalts those of low degree, who fills the hungry and sends the rich away empty, and through her Luke introduces a theme prominent in both the Gospel and Acts. More is involved than the social message and ministry of Jesus in behalf of the oppressed and poor. . . . [H]ere we have a characteristic of the final judgment of God in which there is a complete reversal of fortunes: the powerful and rich will exchange places with the powerless and poor."—Fred B. Craddock, *Luke*, Interpretation, 30.

as sinners, tax collectors, and women, while he is rejected by the "insiders" like the Pharisees, priests, and scribes.

Mary's obedient reply to the God who works impossibilities (1:37; see Gen. 18:14) reverberates with the differences in Gabriel's proclamation about the destinies of the two children (Luke 1:16–17; compare 1:35). In these stories of the prehistory of Jesus and John, their unique respective missions and the contrasts between the two promised children are highlighted. As Luke tells the story, he pulls no punches in declaring that John is subservient to and lesser than Jesus. John will "go before" to "make ready a people prepared for the Lord" (1:17), while Jesus is the "Son of the Most High" and the ruler of a kingdom that will never cease (1:32). God is working God's purposes out in both John and Jesus; both have been expected, but in Jesus the central plan of salvation finds its home and meaning.

Much like throwing a rock into a pond, the announcement stories found in the first pages of Luke's Gospel send forth ripples in all directions. They are ripples that engage the past, highlighting again the providential purposes of God from creation, through the children of Israel, and now in the life of Jesus. The ripples also reach forward into the future, opening up new chapters and new vistas for God's continued salvific actions.

The Meeting of Mary and Elizabeth (1:39–45)

The first step in the unfolding drama of salvation comes in the meeting of Elizabeth and Mary. As the two promise bearers draw together, the past promises of God and the future hopes of salvation lie at the center of their interaction. Alerted by the earlier announcements by Gabriel to Zechariah and Mary, Luke's audience knows that these women carry the "hopes and fears of all the years" within their wombs. Their coming together occasions further expression of God's salvific plan along with the relationship that John and Jesus will have to God's activity.

Luke does not provide any insight into the reason for Mary's journey to see her relative Elizabeth, but upon her arrival powerful signs are given that confirm the uniqueness of the children within the women's respective wombs. Hearing the voice of Mary, the child within Elizabeth's womb leaps in a manner that is later described as a leap of joy (1:44). Fred Craddock harks back to an earlier "leaping" within the womb by suggesting that Luke has tied his audience to yet

another Old Testament story, that of Esau and Jacob in the womb of Rebekah. "The historical allusion is to Rebekah in whose womb Esau and Jacob struggled, the message being in both cases, 'The elder shall serve the younger' (Gen. 25:21–23). The theological point is that prenatal activity, because it precedes all merit or works, witnesses to the sovereign will of God" (Craddock, 29). Following the pattern set earlier in the chapter, the superiority of Jesus to John becomes further established through this historical allusion, where in both cases the blessed child is the younger child.

Mary and Elizabeth

The role of Jesus in God's sovereign plans finds confirmation not only in John's leaping in the womb, but through the greeting that Elizabeth offers Mary. Three pieces of Elizabeth's greeting are of special note: First, much like a prophet under the influence of the spirit of God, Elizabeth calls Mary and her unborn child "blessed." The New Testament scholar Raymond Brown points out that there are two words in Greek that speak to the concept of blessing: one is *makarios,* which is familiar from the Beatitudes ("Blessed are the poor . . .") and suggests a "state of happiness," while the other is *eulogetos,* which "invokes a blessing of God" (Brown, *Birth of the Messiah,* 333). Using the latter word, Elizabeth claims that Mary has been chosen by God, a powerful statement given the social ostracization that would normally have been directed toward an unwed teenage mother-to-be. While spoken about the present situation, Elizabeth's blessing also prophetically looks forward to the fulfillment of this blessing in the life of Mary's unborn child.

Second, Elizabeth signals the identity of the child in Mary's womb by ascribing the title "Lord" to Jesus for one of the first times in Luke—"And why has this happened to me, that the mother of my Lord comes to me?" (1:43; see also the brief reference in 1:17). While this is one of the several designations that are found in Luke in reference to Jesus, the emphasis occurring here ties Jesus to the divine. "Lord" is the term frequently used for the God of Israel (Luke 1:9,

11, 15, 25, 46, 68, etc.), thus connecting Jesus to God and God's plan of salvation. Unlike Matthew, who uses "Lord" to distinguish the faithful from those who misunderstand Jesus, Luke plays on the connection to the divine that the title affirms in Jesus. The title professes the central place of Jesus in God's unfolding plan, in fact equating Jesus to God as participant in and mover of that plan.

Finally, Elizabeth's greeting confirms the appropriate response to God's unfolding plan—hearing and obeying. Earlier, Mary's response to the angel laid the framework for Luke's depiction of faith in Jesus. Elizabeth's final "blessing" toward Mary points again to the significance of the response of faith, a faith in a God who fulfills promises. Using the other word for blessing, *makarios,* Elizabeth confirms the state of happiness that rests with Mary because she has believed that God will fulfill the promises that have been made to her. These words once again paint a picture of faith's response to the unfolding of God's blueprint of salvation; the faithful are those who hear and obey.

Mary's Song (1:46–56)

The focus of the narrative now moves to the mother of the Lord, as Mary breaks forth into a song praising the faithfulness of God. This song, known as the "Magnificat" because of its first word in the Latin translation, has been seen by some scholars to make better sense coming from the mouth of Elizabeth, a reading for which they find support in a few ancient manuscripts and the supposed flow of the narrative. Yet the ascription of the song to Mary carries the weight of the manuscript evidence and the internal sense of the song, as the narrative has clearly identified Mary as the bearer of blessing through Elizabeth's earlier greeting, adding weight to this attestation (see Craddock, 29–30). As with the stories encountered earlier in the first chapter of Luke, Mary's song sends forth ripples that connect it to the past and open up themes that will work themselves out in the narrative that follows. Throughout the Old Testament, key players in the story break forth into song when confronted with the powerful, redemptive activity of God in the face of

---

Mary and Hannah

Mary's song of joy and celebration is often called "The Magnificat" after the first line of the poem: "My soul *magnifies* the Lord, and my spirit rejoices in God my Savior" (Luke 1:46b–47). Compare this with Hannah's words in 1 Samuel 2:1: "My heart exults in the Lord; my strength is exalted in my God. . . ."

overwhelming odds. In response to God's stunning victory at the sea, Moses and Miriam break forth into song that affirms God's glory and power (Exodus 15). In response to an improbable victory over the Canaanites, Deborah declares God's providential care for lowly Israel (Judges 5). In the face of lifelong barrenness, Hannah rejoices in the life-giving power of God that opened her womb and produced Samuel (1 Samuel 2).

Each of these "songs" celebrates the activity of a God who keeps promises in the midst of overwhelming odds. Echoes from these celebrations can be heard in the song Mary now sings in response to Elizabeth's greeting. The closest parallel, however, is to the song of Hannah in response to the birth of Samuel. As we have seen earlier, barrenness is a key theme highlighting the ability of God to work in seemingly impossible situations. The narratives in 1 Samuel indicate the barrenness of Hannah and the remarkable melody that she sings in response to God's life-giving action that results in the birth of Samuel. Hannah has gone from barren and empty to life-giver, from a second-class citizen in a society that held the bearing of male children in high esteem to the mother of a firstborn son; that is, from death to new life. This reversal of fortune is clearly sounded in her words:

> The bows of the mighty are broken,
>   but the feeble gird on strength.
> Those who were full have hired themselves out for bread,
>   but those who were hungry are fat with spoil.
> The barren has borne seven,
>   but she who has many children is forlorn.
>
> (1 Sam. 2:4–5)

"That she should sing this song that links God's blessing of her in her 'lowliness' to God's promises for the whole people makes Mary into the lead singer in a chorus of all those whose dreams and yearnings are given voice in its words."—Sharon H. Ringe, *Luke*, Westminster Bible Companion, 34.

Hannah celebrates the implosion of grace into the world that turns the world upside down.

In Luke, Mary also celebrates the effects of God's grace impacting human history through the child that she now bears in her womb. Her song can be broken down into two stanzas, verses 46–49 and verses 50–55. The first stanza focuses on Mary and recalls the statements that have been made about her by Elizabeth. Praising God with names that will become attached to the child in her womb, Lord and Savior (1:46–47), Mary celebrates her unique role in God's purposes for creation. Her self-characterization, which moves from lowly servant to one called blessed by all generations, recalls the reversals that God worked in Hannah's story, and also sets the stage for the coming events that will continue to turn the world upside down. As Fred Craddock notes, what happens to Mary is already "evidence" for the "eschatological reversals" that will be characteristic of Luke's description of God's activity within history (Craddock, 30).

The second stanza of Mary's song centers on God's merciful power and how that power intertwines with human history. Mary begins this stanza with a word that refers to a central characteristic of God, translated mercy, or steadfast love, which an audience familiar with the Old Testament would have known quite well. From the repeating refrain of Psalm 136, ". . . the *steadfast love* of the LORD endures forever," to the classic formulation of Exodus 34:6–7, "The LORD, the LORD . . . abounding in *steadfast love* . . . keeping *steadfast love* for the thousandth generation," the mercy/steadfast love of God is a central tenet of the faith of the Old Testament that Mary now highlights and connects to the next generation. In fact, God's mercy brackets the second stanza of Mary's song, setting the context in which the following verses are to be understood (v. 50) and providing the summary statement for the action of God that these verses describe (v. 54). Central to Luke's Gospel is the understanding that everything described therein arises out of the mercy of God, a theme stated directly here in Mary's song.

What is the impact of the mercy of God on human history? Following the opening proclamation of God's faithfulness, Mary describes the effects of God's mercy through a series of reversals of fortune, which will become thematic for Luke. The poetry of this section is finely tuned, so that many have seen the hint of a chiasmus. This poetic figure, using the structure ABCCBA and especially suited for showing reversals, shows forth the turnabouts that God has wrought and will continue to bring forth in history:

> He has shown strength with his arm; (A)
> > he has scattered the proud in the thoughts of their hearts.
> > He has brought down the powerful from their thrones, (B)
> > > and lifted up the lowly; (C)
> > > he has filled the hungry with good things, (C₁)
> > and sent the rich away empty. (B₁)
> He has helped his servant Israel. . . . (A₁)
> > > > > > (Luke 1:51–54a)

Bracketed by the parallel concepts of showing strength and helping, the inner verses highlight the transpositions that the mercy of God exacts from history. Those who are proud, powerful, and rich find themselves scattered, brought down, and sent away empty, while those who are lowly and hungry are lifted up and filled. These reversals, which turn the order of the world upside down, set the theme of salvation that is described in Luke's Gospel—the restoring of right relationships, the lifting up of the estranged (i.e., women, the poor, tax collectors, etc.), and the humbling of the proud. The salvation of God disrupts the orders of the world, healing and making some whole while challenging and humbling others.

Two features of Mary's description of God's activity deserve further note. First, the verbs used to portray this action occur in the past tense. The use of this particular past tense suggests that the events wrought by God's mercy are completed and, in a sense, timeless. The present and the future are ensured by the past. Even though the song points toward the future activity to be concluded in Jesus, "So sure is the singer that God will do what is promised that it is proclaimed as an accomplished fact" (Craddock, 30).

> Mary's song "speaks of three of the revolutions of God. (i) *He scatters the proud in the plans of their hearts.* This is a *moral* revolution. Christianity is the death of pride. . . . (ii) *He casts down the mighty— he exalts the humble.* That is a *social* revolution. Christianity puts an end to the world's labels and prestige. . . . (iii) *He has filled those who are hungry . . . those who are rich he has sent empty away.* That is an *economic* revolution. . . . There is loveliness in the *Magnificat* but in that loveliness there is dynamite. Christianity begets a revolution in each man and revolution in the world."—William Barclay, *The Gospel of Luke*, Daily Study Bible, 15–16.

Second, the shifts in status between the rich and the poor should not be seen as an occasion of rejoicing that the rich will finally receive their just deserts. It is important to recognize how the framing celebration of God's mercy and the center describing the reversal of fortunes interpret each other. Within the frame of God's mercy, the center loses any tone of vengeance or triumphalism. Instead, a world marked by scarcity and competition is replaced by a world of generosity in which all have enough: Those who are hungry now enjoy good things, and those who are rich do not add to their riches. The powerful no longer exercise power over others, but nothing is said about the "lowly" now doing what has been done to them (Ringe, 33).

Mary completes her song with the closing reference to the mercy of God, but now ties God's mercy to God's remembering. Here again, the introductory words of Luke's Gospel pick up and elaborate a theme common from the Old Testament, the memory of God. In the central salvation story of the Old Testament, the freeing of the Hebrew slaves from the Egyptian pharaoh, one of the crucial factors behind the redemptive activity of God is God's remembering the covenantal promises made earlier to Abraham and his kin: "God heard their groaning, and God remembered his covenant with Abraham, Issac, and Jacob" (Ex. 2:24; see also Ex. 6:5; Lev. 26:42, 45; and Ps. 105:8ff.). Likewise, the psalmist proclaims that God's memory is central to understanding God's mercy and God's action on behalf of the oppressed and

> ### 📖 Want to Know More?
>
> **About songs of praise?** See Jerome F. D. Creach, *Psalms*, Interpretation Bible Studies, especially pp. 2, 13–21.
>
> **About women in the time of Jesus?** See Carol A. Newsom and Sharon H. Ringe, eds., *Women's Bible Commentary*, expanded ed. (Louisville, Ky.: Westminster John Knox Press, 1998), 251–59, 482–88.

distressed: "For their sake he remembered his covenant, and showed compassion according to the abundance of his steadfast love" (Ps. 106:45; see also Pss. 89:47, 50; 98:3; 136:23). Thus, Mary's song closes with a definitive statement of God's long-standing memory, which connects the current situation of a mother bearing a child with the continued unfolding of God's plan for the world, a plan that is tied to the ancient history of Abraham's people.

As Luke tells the story, the birth proclaimed in these passages sent ripples through human history. Jesus' birth spotlights God's past activity, while moving forward to shine the light of God's salvific plan on the future. For Luke, God has been, God is, and God will be active in the world. The question is, can we make the connections so that we too may hear and obey?

❓ Questions for Reflection

1. Compare Luke 1:46–55 to 1 Samuel 2:1–10. In what way are these passages similar? How are they different? In what ways are the women who spoke these words alike?
2. The writer of this passage used the past tense to describe God's mercy. Why is this significant?

3. What is the significance of Luke's beginning his narrative with the stories of two women, both of them barren? Recall the stories of Abraham and Sarah (Genesis 16), Jacob and Rachel (Gen. 29:31–30:24), and Elkanah and Hannah (1 Sam. 1:5–20).

4. The mother of Jesus was an unwed teenager. Is this an aspect of Mary that Christians today are prone to ignore or downplay? What does God's choice of Mary teach us about God?

2

The Temptations:
Who Is Jesus, Part One

> During the past two thousand years, few issues if any have so persis-
> tently brought out the fundamental assumptions of each epoch as has
> the attempt to come to terms with the meaning of the figure of Jesus
> of Nazareth.
>
> —Jaroslav Pelikan

Who is Jesus? As the quote from Jaroslav Pelikan suggests, that question and the variety of answers it has spawned have been on minds for centuries. During each period of time, an attempt is made to understand Jesus in light of the particularity of that period's circumstances, so that the Christ is interpreted through the images, both biblical and nonbiblical, available within the culture of the day. While these interactions of the "culture of the day" and the traditions surrounding Jesus serve to keep the image of Jesus alive and engaged, Pelikan's observation notes that Jesus is often portrayed through the cultural assumptions of the day. In other words, we reconstruct Jesus in our image, as our preconceptions and preferences shape our understandings of the Christ. As when we look in a mirror or paint a self-portrait, we create a Jesus conformed to our image instead of the reverse: our being created and conformed to him as the living God. From the beginnings of God's relationship with the covenant people, the danger inherent in this idolatrous process has been known through the prohibitions found in the early commandments against worshiping other gods and graven images (Ex. 20:1–4; Deut. 5:6–10).

After the first three chapters of Luke introduce Jesus, Luke moves to answer the question of Jesus' identity directly in the next major section of the material, Luke 4:1–9:50, which is often referred to as Jesus' Galilean ministry. Within these chapters that focus on Jesus' healing and preaching in Galilee, Luke provides an examination of the nature and character of Jesus ministry. Each of the stories focuses Luke's audience on the uniqueness of Jesus and how that uniqueness plays itself out in the particular moments of Jesus' early ministry. Through this telling Luke confronts his audience with the "real" Jesus so that their preconceptions are named and eventually melted away.

Setting the Stage

Immediately prior to Luke 4, Luke provides two stories that prepare the reader for Jesus' ministry. The first piece of information comes from the baptismal story of Jesus. Unlike Matthew, Mark, and John, who record John as baptizing Jesus, Luke tells the story of the baptism after reporting John's arrest (3:19), suggesting that John had not been present at Jesus baptism. While it is difficult to know why Luke relates the story in this manner, he has consistently elevated Jesus' ministry above John's so that they never seem to share the stage directly together. For Luke, John and Jesus are intertwined, but their connection never overshadows Jesus as the "coming one."

"You are my son, the Beloved."

Luke provides only the barest description of Jesus' baptism, noting that he was baptized with others. Yet in the midst of this scene, Jesus prays. In Luke's Gospel, prayer becomes a "marker event" calling attention to a turning point or critical moment in the story, as Jesus often moves away from the stage to pray at strategic junctures in the narrative (see 5:16; 6:12; 9:18, 29; 11:1; 22:19). In the baptismal scene, Jesus' prayer coincides with the opening of the heavens and the descent of the Holy Spirit accompanied by a voice proclaiming, "You are my Son, the Beloved; with you I am well pleased" (3:22). This baptismal event makes two vigorous claims about Jesus: his life and ministry are infused by the Holy Spirit, and he is the "son of God." Luke has already mentioned both of these themes in the earlier stories surrounding the birth of Jesus (e.g., Gabriel's announcement to Mary in 1:35 that also combines the concepts of the Spirit and Son of God), but now they appear for the first time directly associated with the person of Jesus. The rest of the narrative will work out Jesus' relation to the Spirit and his identity as the son of God.

Following the baptism, Luke provides the genealogy of Jesus (3:23–38). There are easily detectable differences between Luke's genealogy and Matthew's (Matt. 1:1–18), since both of these writers use this material in distinct ways. Matthew intentionally connects Jesus to the story of Israel, highlighting his lineage and relationship to the promise networks surrounding David and Abraham. Luke, on the other hand, presents the genealogical material in such a way as to connect Jesus to the first human person, Adam. Although Abraham and David are mentioned in Luke's genealogy, they do not occupy as prominent a place as they do in Matthew's narrative. For Luke, Jesus is part of God's purpose for creation from the dawn of time, so he traces Jesus' roots directly to the first human. God's unfolding drama connects Jesus intimately to the human condition and human beings. Tracing Jesus' line back to Adam also allows for a reiteration of the claim that Jesus is the son of God (1:38), a claim that will be further defined and delineated in the stories that follow.

The Temptations (4:1–13)

Up to this point, Luke has laid the framework for understanding Jesus indirectly—that is, through other characters speaking about Jesus—except for the encounter in the Temple at age twelve (2:41–52), which gives only the briefest glimpse into his nature. Beginning with 4:1 and following, Luke adds flesh to the bones of his framework as he moves Jesus into center stage of the story. Jesus becomes the primary actor on the stage, so that his words and actions play central roles in highlighting and portraying the key import of his identity. Like someone introducing an honored speaker, Luke has laid the groundwork for Jesus through the various testimonies given in the birth and infancy stories. Now it is time for the speaker to come to the podium, the central protagonist to come onstage, and time for the audience to encounter the "real McCoy."

Like any good introduction, Luke's prefatory material has built expectations concerning Jesus. These expectations, both those of Luke's original audiences and ours, become the lens through which Luke throws light on his understanding of the true identity of Jesus. In the material that follows, the preconceptions that surround our understanding of Jesus are peeled away so that again and anew we encounter Jesus, his ministry, and the call it places upon our lives. The material that follows serves as a refiner's fire, removing false hopes and expectations, destroying each "little Jesus" that we have constructed in our own image, and presenting again the unique and radical claim that Jesus is God's son. By prefacing Luke 4 with the baptismal story of Jesus, however, Luke also informs his reader that what follows concerns a question of identity centered within the person of Jesus himself. What does it mean for Jesus that he is the Beloved son, with whom God is well pleased? How will Jesus act and be in the world as the chosen one, the Son of God?

Luke begins these verses of identity clarification with a direct tie to the preceding passages by proclaiming that the Spirit leads Jesus into the wilderness. For an audience familiar with the variety of stories in the Old Testament about time in the wilderness (see Exodus 16; Numbers 11; and 1 Kings 19), it comes as no surprise that during Jesus' time there a tempting or a testing would occur. As with the people of ancient Israel, Jesus is not left alone to wander the wilderness, but is accompanied and even led in the journey by the Spirit. This presence, however, did not protect Jesus from the trials that lay ahead, as Fred Craddock notes. "Nor did the presence of the Holy Spirit mean the absence of temptation: rather, the Spirit was the available power of God in the contest" (Craddock, 55).

> "If anyone is having trouble believing that Jesus was *really* tempted, then he or she needs to keep in mind that temptation is an indication of strength, not of weakness. We are not tempted to do what we cannot do but what is within our power. The greater the strength, the greater the temptation."—Fred B. Craddock, *Luke*, Interpretation, 56.

The climactic contest between the devil and Jesus begins after his forty-day sojourn without food, so that Jesus finds himself in a famished condition (Luke 4:2). With Jesus in this depleted condition, the devil engages the high gear and tests him. Moving through the temptations, it is important to note that for something to truly be tempting it must be possible; that is, we are tempted toward that which is possible and not that which is impossible. Most of us are not tempted literally to fly to the moon, because for most of us that is not a real possibility. Furthermore, temptation appears in a pleasing form rather than an ugly form of "evil." No one is tempted to commit adultery by hearing a voice saying this will destroy you, your spouse, your kids, possibly your job, your close friendships, and so forth. No, the voice of temptation focuses on the supposed pleasure and the excitement, the suspense and the thrill. Finally, ultimate temptations are those that tempt us to do good, to provide help, or to act on another's behalf. Any parent who has ever taught a child to ride a bike knows how tempting it can be to keep holding on so that the child remains steady, but eventually the parent has to let go so that the child can ride. "All this is to say that a real temptation is an offer not to fall but to rise" (Craddock, 56).

In the verses that follow, the devil offers Jesus three "real" temptations, meaning they are possible, pleasant, and apparently for the good of all. In the first place, Jesus is tempted to turn a stone into bread in order to feed himself. The devil ties this temptation to the sonship of Jesus, saying, "If you are the Son of God . . ." Later in Luke's Gospel, Jesus miraculously feeds five thousand with five loaves and two fishes (9:12–17), so the possibility exists for Jesus to achieve this material change. The sound of food after forty days of fasting makes the offer pleasing, but it is the possibilities that the transformation of the stone to bread offer that strike to the core of this temptation. Given the persistent problems of hunger that continue to beset our world today, the devil's temptation does not fall on deaf ears. Would it not be wonderful to solve the problems of world hunger through a snap of Jesus' fingers? There are more than enough stones in the world for loaves galore. Deep inside Luke's audience, the temptation becomes real as well.

Jesus responds to the temptation by quoting from Deuteronomy 8:3: "Human beings shall not live by bread alone." Arising from a summary statement given by Moses as the children of Israel stand on the border of the promised land, this quote points to the sustenance that arises from God and the importance of trusting that God will provide. In Deuteronomy 8, Moses reminds Israel that God's care was so plentiful during their wilderness wanderings that their clothes did not wear out and their feet did not swell after forty years of walking (Deut. 8:4). Later, Jesus will remind his followers not to be anxious about what they shall eat or wear (Luke 12:22–31), but to seek the kingdom of God, for God will provide. In the face of the tempter, Jesus draws on the tradition of his faith to declare that grasping for social gain, for "bread," leads to forgetfulness, lack of trust, and eventually death (Deut. 8:17–20).

Next, the devil takes Jesus up and shows him all the kingdoms of the world and in effect offers Jesus the keys to the kingdoms: "To you I will give their glory and all this authority; for it has been given over to me, and I give it to anyone I please. If you, then, will worship me, it will all be yours" (Luke 4:6–7). Imagine Jesus controlling all the kingdoms of the world. Imagine Jesus being the head of state and guiding the world under his auspices and his rule. Imagine justice, peace, mercy, love, all the central characteristics of Jesus rolled into political power and processes. Again, Luke's audience hears this temptation as tantalizingly seductive, so that we imagine how the world would be if Jesus accepted the offer.

There is one condition, however, and it is that Jesus must bow down and worship the tempter. Given the good that will come out of Jesus' reign, this small detail does not seem to matter. Yet here again Jesus responds to the test by quoting from Deuteronomy 6:13, firmly stating an allegiance to God and God alone. This piece of the ancient tradition comes immediately after the central claim of Israel's faith, the *shema* in Deuteronomy 6:4–5: "Hear, O Israel: the LORD is our God, the Lord alone. You shall love the LORD your God with all your heart, and with all your soul, and with all your might." Deuteronomy 6 goes on to remind the children of God that God is a jealous God who brooks no rivals. According to the ancient tradition, worship of anyone or anything besides God is futile, because there is no equal to God. Once again in the face of the tempter, Jesus draws on the ancient tradition to combat the tempter's lure, a lure here that is to easy power and cheap authority. For as the story goes, Jesus is proclaimed king by his executioners as they hang a sign on his cross declaring in three languages that he is king. Jesus, ever obedient and worshiping God alone, does inherit the kingdoms, but in a totally different manner than the tempter offers, in a costly manner of obedience and sacrificial denial.

> "In the pages of scripture, Satan is a metaphor for evil, or in literary terms, a personification that draws into one mythical being all the images and concepts theorized about evil by the Israelites throughout their history. He represents the existence of evil both in people and the world. His role should be taken seriously because something is radically wrong with the perspectives and actions of people."—Alyce M. McKenzie, *Matthew*, Interpretation Bible Studies, 26.

Finally, the devil takes Jesus to Jerusalem and invites him to prove his unique father-son relationship with God by jumping off the Temple wall. At this point, the order of the temptations in Matthew and Luke is different, as the order of the last two temptations is reversed for Matthew. In Luke's version, the order of the last two temptations fits within the significance that is placed on Jerusalem as the focal point of God's salvation history. The Gospel begins (1:5ff.) and ends (24:52–53) at worship in the Temple of Jerusalem, while Luke tells the story of the spread of the gospel as a dispersion of hope from Jerusalem in the book of Acts. The tempter brings Jesus to Jerusalem, the center point, and invites Jesus to begin his ministry with an awesome deed of power. Perhaps seeing how Jesus has relied on the ancient scriptural tradition to overcome the earlier tests, the tempter now offers not only a new possibility, but scriptural warrant for this proposal by quoting Psalm 91. In citing God's protective power, the devil encourages Jesus to prove once and for all that he is God's son by performing an amazing miracle.

The demand for proof has not changed much in the two thousand years that have passed since these first temptations. We are fascinated by the "miraculous" and desire tangible and visible evidence of the awesome power of God. From our ancient ancestor Jacob who, even after encountering the powerful dream of the ladder, played the game of "God, if you do this for me, then I will believe you" (Gen. 28:20), to Jesus' own townspeople, who wanted a demonstration of his power in their streets (Luke 4:23ff.), the children of God have always sought proof beyond the readily apparent. We would like to make such demands upon God as we face the vagaries of human life, the difficulties of balancing job and family, the big algebra test, or the diagnosis of illness in a dear loved one. "God, if you are God, then do something about . . ." The tempter was not the first, nor will he be the last, to ask for a demonstration of God's power for belief.

Jesus, however, remains true to the identity that has been evident from the first temptation. Drawing from the deep well of his scriptural tradition, he answers the tempter once more with a quote from Deuteronomy, this time Deuteronomy 6:16: "Do not put the LORD your God to the test." Jesus taps into the wilderness story of ancient Israel yet another time, as he quotes from a passage about the Israelites' complaining desires for water in the wilderness. Despite the sustenance they had been receiving, the people of Israel desired further proof, saying, "Is the LORD among us or not?" (Ex. 17:7). Yet as seen earlier in the Deuteronomy texts, God provided and provided more than enough through the wanderings, so that once again Jesus couches his response in such a way as to emphasize his trust in God and God's providential care. Following this final rebuttal, Luke notes that the devil departs from Jesus until an opportune time comes for further testing. (See Luke 22:3, where the devil reappears.)

Before moving on, three observations are worth noting. First, Jesus is not left without resources to fight the tempter. He draws upon the vast testimony of his tradition. In the first three chapters of his

Gospel, Luke informs us that Jesus has been raised in line with the Jewish customs of his day: circumcised on the eighth day (Luke 2:21), presented to God in the following weeks (Luke 2:22), practiced in the rituals as his family customarily journeyed to Jerusalem for the festivals (Luke 2:41). Entering the contest with the devil, he is steeped in the tradition and given ammunition for the battle that ensues. Luke is clear that the pattern of Jesus' childhood and his upbringing within the tradition have given Jesus the spiritual assets to face the trials that lie ahead.

Second, these early temptations of Jesus remain with us today. We continue to find ourselves pushing an identity upon Jesus and trying to fit him within our social, religious, or political agendas (see Craddock, 56, for these aspects of the temptations). We make Jesus part of our cause, instead of trusting in God's care and guidance for the world. Interestingly, one scholar has noted that Jesus' temptations in Luke are in the reverse order of the first three petitions of the Lord's Prayer: Hallowed be thy name; thy kingdom come, thy will be done; give us this day our daily bread (Fitzmyer, 507). Our petitions easily turn into temptations when we try to manipulate God for our purposes, but are petitions when they rely on God's providence, mercy, and grace. Finally, in each of the three temptations Jesus has been tempted to declare what it means to be the "son of God," so that his rejection of each temptation holds open the question of who he will be. As Sharon Ringe has noted, each temptation serves as a negation— "Jesus is not going to be . . ."—but it does not give any positive indications of who Jesus will be or definitive descriptions of his activity as the son of God (Ringe, 61). This is left for the material that follows.

> "By assuring us that the same Spirit that filled Jesus and led him into the wilderness (4:1) filled him also at the end of the time in the wilderness, Luke is not only closing the parentheses around this episode. He is also assuring us that Jesus is equipped for the more subtle challenges and more difficult days ahead."—Sharon H. Ringe, *Luke,* Westminster Bible Companion, 61.

The True Nature of Jesus' Ministry (4:14–21)

Continuing under the guidance of the Spirit, Jesus returns to Galilee and travels through the region. Reports concerning Jesus spread out through the land, so that his fame increases. Unlike Matthew and Mark, who link the beginning of Jesus' ministry with a call to repentance and the coming of the kingdom of God (Matt. 4:17; Mark 1:15), Luke reveals that Jesus moves throughout Galilee teaching in the synagogues and being "glorified" by all he encounters (Luke 4:15). Luke provides further clarification of Jesus' role and ministry in the encounter that follows, as Jesus returns home and goes to his hometown synagogue.

As with the earlier narratives of chapters 1–3, Luke reminds his readers right away that Jesus sits firmly in the midst of Jewish customs and traditions. Following the report within the temptation stories claiming that Jesus' understanding and participation in his tradition provided him the resources to confront the tempter, the narrative reports that Jesus remains firmly rooted as he goes to the synagogue to worship, as is his custom (Luke 4:16). Jesus has roots and these roots provide him sustenance for life in the midst of the seductions of the world and the lures to be someone other than the one whom God has proclaimed and affirmed at Jesus' baptism.

Entering the synagogue, Jesus proceeds to read from the Isaiah scroll that is handed to him. Jesus has assumed center stage in Luke's narrative and stands to read from the scriptural tradition that has supported him in the earlier time of his testing. Intriguingly, every word that Jesus has spoken until this point in chapter 4 has been a quotation from scripture, and that trend continues, further tying Jesus to his heritage and the salvific plan revealed through Israel's scriptures. Building on the aspects of trust in God that the earlier quotations reveal, Jesus now reads a passage that will become paradigmatic for his ministry. Read in sequence, the play with the quotations and their structure in Luke 4 moves from a bold proclamation of God's enduring faithfulness to life in response to that faithfulness.

Luke's text here, however, is ambiguous, for the reader is left unaware whether Jesus chooses the passage from which he reads or reads the passage for the day. In either case, Jesus reads: "The Spirit of the Lord is upon me, because he has anointed me to bring good news to the poor. He has sent me to proclaim release to the captives and recovering of sight to the blind, to let the oppressed go free, to proclaim the year of the Lord's favor" (Luke 4:18–19).

These verses come from Isaiah 61:1–2, adding a piece from Isaiah 58:6. Following his pronouncement, Jesus sits down and draws the attention of all those who have assembled in the synagogue. Throughout his Gospel, Luke reports that those who encounter the teaching of Jesus are amazed and caught up in wonderment. It is no different here, as the text builds in anticipation of the first words that

Jesus will speak in chapter 4 that are not a direct quotation from scripture: "Today this scripture has been fulfilled in your hearing" (Luke 4:21). After the temptations that try to pull Jesus away from his central identity, Jesus proclaims in his hometown synagogue the preeminent nature of his ministry, which he couches in the terms of the fulfillment of these prophecies from the Isaiah scroll. In between references to fulfillment—the introduction to Theophilus (1:1–4) and the road to Emmaus (24:27)—the spotlight shines intensely on Jesus as he is the fulfillment and fulcrum of God's action with human beings.

As the centerpiece of God's action, Jesus declares that he redeems and turns the world upside down for those who have been abandoned, exploited, and burdened: the poor, blind, the captives, and the oppressed. Under the anointing power of the Spirit, Jesus' proclamation of the good news of release, recovery, and liberty demonstrates the dominant transaction of God's salvific work within humanity—lifting up and restoring—that will be seen in the coming narratives about Jesus' Galilean ministry (Luke 4:31–9:51; see the next unit for a fuller exploration of these themes). The picture of the reversal of fortunes of the forgotten and exploited receives a final brush stroke in the last line of Jesus' reading where he mentions the "year of the Lord's favor," which most scholars believe to be a reference to the Jubilee year described in Leviticus 25. The Jubilee year was part of the overarching tradition surrounding sabbath practice, the year after seven periods of seven years (i.e., the 50th year), in which every portion of Israel's lands is returned to its original family allotment from the time of Israel's entrance to the land. While there is no recorded instance that Israel ever practiced this economic restructuring, the Jubilee year was grounded in the idea that all the land was a gift from God and thus ultimately belonged to God. In theory, the Jubilee would have been a way to prevent a permanent underclass, as new generations would get new starts and not be saddled with the burdens of their ancestors. Jesus, the embodiment of the Jubilee, now announces a new beginning, so that the last will be treated like the first and the first like the last.

The Reaction of the Hometown (4:22–30)

Jesus has returned home, has spoken with authority about his identity, and now his hometown folks are amazed. The crowd is abuzz with conversation, as one neighbor turns to the next: "Is this not

Joseph's son?" (Luke 4:22). The people claim him as one of their own. Flush with the revelation of Jesus' identity, they stake their claim: "He's our boy. One of Nazareth's own. Wow! We've heard what he has done elsewhere, what will he do here!" Luke does not actually report these words, but Jesus' reaction to the crowd's murmurs reveals that his hometown folks want to get their hooks into Jesus and benefit from his presence. The crowd feels that they are privileged and will receive an inordinate amount of blessings, because Jesus is one of their own.

In response to these suppositions, Jesus pulls on the heritage and tradition that he shares with the hometown crowd. Recalling the stories of two of the premier prophets in ancient Israel, Elijah and Elisha, Jesus reminds his neighbors that they have no special hold or power over him. During a famine Elijah aided a foreign woman from Zarephath while Israel suffered (1 Kings 17:9). Likewise, although there were many lepers in Israel, Elisha healed the Syrian leader, Naaman, of his leprosy (2 Kings 5:1ff.). The townspeople believe that because they are "his" people, they will find themselves in a special position of privilege and prestige. Jesus reminds this crowd, and all those who want to possess and control him by limiting his grace to their inner circle, that God's redemptive power is not limited in its provenance, leaping across borders and boundaries. Faced with their comeuppance, the crowd becomes angry and tries to kill Jesus, foreshadowing the rejection and actual killing that come later (4:29–30).

Much like the devil in 4:1–13, the townspeople try to manipulate and control the identity of Jesus. They want to put him a box, the box of special privilege, which would ensure them of their cherished place and a unique portion of Jesus' power. Like the devil before them, they try to cast an identity on Jesus despite hearing his definitive declaration of who he was.

Want to Know More?

About Satan? See Shirley C. Guthrie, *Christian Doctrine*, rev. ed. (Louisville, Ky.: Westminster John Knox Press, 1994), 166–91, especially 179–82.

About John the Baptist? See Paul J. Achtemeier, ed., HarperCollins Bible Dictionary, rev. ed. (San Francisco: HarperSanFrancisco, 1996), 538–39.

About temptation in the Gospels? See Alyce M. McKenzie, *Matthew*, Interpretation Bible Studies, 21–27.

About the baptism of Jesus? For a thorough discussion on the historic understandings of the reasons for Jesus' baptism, see George R. Beasley-Murray, *Baptism in the New Testament* (Grand Rapids: Wm. B. Eerdmans Publishing Co., 1973), 45–67.

On the old game show *To Tell the Truth*, after the celebrities had asked their questions of the three people all claiming to be one person and had cast their votes for the one they believed to be the "real McCoy," the announcer would proclaim, "Will the real Bill Smith please stand up?" In these stories from the beginning of Jesus' Galilean ministry, Luke has had the real Jesus stand up, so that the impostors, the images of Jesus formed by the devil, the townspeople, and even by us, are ushered offstage. The narrative has introduced the "real McCoy," and against it all attempts to describe Jesus must be measured and held to account.

? Questions for Reflection

1. Fred Craddock writes that "a real temptation is an offer not to fall but to rise." What does he mean by this? Have you experienced this type of temptation to rise?
2. This passage helps destroy some of the "little Jesuses" that we have built in our minds. What does that mean? Do you have any "little Jesuses?"
3. If Satan placed three temptations before us today, what would they be? Where are we spiritually vulnerable?
4. Are we sometimes like the devil, demanding proof of the authenticity of Jesus? How so?

3

The Galilean Ministry: Who Is Jesus, Part Two

It seems that everyone enjoys a good mystery. From Sherlock Holmes to P. D. James, there seems to be an innate fascination with the riddles of the unknown and the search for answers. In any mystery or detective story, one of the key elements of the narrative art centers on the provision of clues and hints that either lead or mislead the audience toward a resolution. Engaging the narrative, the audience looks for and pays attention to the clues that are given in order to piece together enough evidence to solve the crime and discern the identity of the culprit. There are moments when the clues are straightforward, blatant, and easy to spot, while other clues remain buried in the text and require insightful extraction. Once the clues have been gathered, the synapses connected, the prize of figuring out "who done it" awaits the careful reader.

For children growing up today, it seems that the love of mysteries remains, so that paying attention to clues is still an important skill to learn. One of the most popular children's programs on TV today is called *Blue's Clues,* a program about a young man named Steve and his dog, Blue. On each program, Blue desires something but, being a dog, cannot come out directly and identify the game she wants to play, the story she wants read, or the treat she has in mind. So Blue marks clues with a blue pawprint and as the show moves on, these clues are found. Observing a four-year-old watching this program is great fun, because Steve never seems to notice the clue right away, but the child does. At approximately the same time that the child sitting at home notices Blue's pawprint, childrens' voices offscreen begin shouting "A clue! A clue!" Steve runs at the camera until his face fills the screen, saying "What? You see a clue? Where, where is the clue?" Of course, the four-year-old participates along with the offscreen voices, as they run to the screen and proudly point to an apple, a book, or a plane with a blue pawprint on it saying, "There! There! There's the clue!" By the end of the show, Steve and his eager audience have gathered their clues and retired to the "Thinking Chair" to figure out what Blue is after. This engaging television show teaches children to be perceptive and to pay attention to the clues that exist around them.

Looking for Clues

At the beginning of his Gospel, Luke suggests that all the verses that follow are clues to the identity of Jesus (Luke 1:1–4). We have seen that these introductory verses in Luke's Gospel set the stage for the material that follows, as the Gospel purports to be an "orderly account of the events that have been fulfilled among us," so that Theophilus might "know the truth." Within the first nine chapters of Luke's Gospel, the central focus of the quest for truth rests in the identity of Jesus. Luke has scattered his Gospel with hints, traces, suggestions, and in places blatant statements, all of which point to discerning the answer to the central question "Who is Jesus?" In fact, each story in the Gospel, from the announcement of Jesus' birth by the angels to the shepherds (Luke 2:14–15), to the questions from John about others casting out demons in Jesus' name (Luke 9:49–50), provides insight into this crucial question. The question of Jesus' identity never retreats far from those who engage Luke, but it is most clearly examined in the early chapters (chaps. 1–9).

One of the unique things about this early part of Luke's Gospel is the number of times characters in the narrative actually ponder the question, "Who is this person?" Perhaps in no other Gospel do we meet as many people who ask the question, "Who is this?" Many people, when confronted with Jesus, found themselves wondering, questioning, and exploring. These stories are clues in the narrative that are none too subtle. Where other places in the narrative point to the identity of Jesus at times indirectly, here Luke seems to be placing a big blue pawprint on the page and saying, "A clue! A clue!" Pay attention to how the question is answered. These texts are blunt and straightforward in giving answers—"This is who Jesus is."

"Is not this Joseph's son?" (4:22)

At the beginning of his ministry, Jesus returns home to Nazareth. On the Sabbath he goes to the synagogue, and there he reads powerful words from the scroll of Isaiah about restoring sight, healing infirmities, and good news for the poor. After finishing the scroll, Jesus sits down amid the elders and says, "Today this scripture has been fulfilled in your hearing." And then it happens. The murmurs start in the crowd. One person turns to the next and says "Who is this? Who is this one? Who is this one who talks about the fulfillment of God's prophecies, about restoring sight, removing bonds?" From the people of his hometown of Nazareth—who marvel at his wisdom and wonder "Who is this?"—the answer eventually arises: "We know who this is. He looks so familiar. Isn't he Joseph's son? Yes, this is the carpenter's son from down the way. Don't you remember him and what he did to his parents when he was twelve? Oh yes, that's who this is." Yet, given what Jesus has said and done, we know this is a clue. It is a clue about the identity of Jesus, who is more than just Joseph's son—he is the fulfillment of prophecies about God's restorative plans for the world. We have seen that the crowds of his hometown expected Jesus to be one thing; yet he was much more. Luke has set the stage for unpacking the identity of Jesus and will provide us more clues as we continue through the narrative.

"Who can forgive sins but God alone?" (5:17–26)

In the next chapter of Luke, we find Jesus teaching in a house packed with the local people and with religious leaders who, we are told, have come from far and wide to hear Jesus. It is no surprise that Jesus would draw a crowd of these leaders, as they would be interested in any new interpretations of their religious heritage and possibly the emergence of a new rabbi or teacher of wisdom. While Jesus is teaching, some men arrive with a friend who was paralyzed and could not make it in through the front door because of the crowd. Finally, they remove tiles from the roof and lower their friend on a pallet right in front of Jesus. Impressed by the faith of this intrepid band, Jesus proclaims that the man's sins are forgiven.

Then it comes—Luke puts the pawprint on the page again, as we hear some of the Pharisees and religious leaders begin the murmur: "Who is this? Who does this guy think he is? Only God can forgive sins! Does he think he's God? Who is this?" By raising the questions through the Pharisees, Luke tells us to pay attention to this text as a clue about the identity of Jesus. The Pharisees had expected only a teacher of wisdom, a wise rabbi, but what they expected and what they found were vastly different. Here was one who claimed the authority to heal and forgive, related powers that the Jewish people reserved for God alone. (See Ex. 15:26; Deut. 32:39; Ps. 103:3. In the Old Testament, healing and forgiveness are often seen as parallel concepts, a worldview out of which Jesus appears to be operating here, according to Luke.) In Nazareth, Jesus describes his future ministry in terms of release; here Luke tells us that Jesus operates with the power of God to release those bound by their sins and diseases, a holistic picture of the restorative power of God that is often lost in our compartmentalized understanding of human beings that separates body, soul, spirit, and mind. Through the questions of the Pharisees, we see that Jesus embodies the power of God to act on behalf of "whole persons," not just their religious/spiritual parts (see Craddock, 128).

"Are you the one?" (7:18–22)

"There is enough misery in the world to make the message that a Messiah *will* come believable; there is enough misery in the world to make the message that a Messiah *has* come unbelievable. The first and major task of a Messiah is to get people to quit looking for one."—Fred B. Craddock, *Luke,* Interpretation, 127.

As the story progresses, Luke continues to paint the picture of Jesus acting on behalf of the persons he encounters, so much so that his fame begins to spread. The news of Jesus' activity even reaches John the Baptist in prison. This text (7:18ff.) has as an implicit background: John's prison experience. John finds himself unjustly imprisoned by Herod as one suspected of stirring up sedition against the king. Unless you have been part of a prison, it is difficult to imagine a place where life is controlled by outside forces, where for some there is the possibility of torture and death, where fear and anxiety are part of the daily routine. Victor Frankl, a survivor of a concentration camp in World War II, has written about his experience of being locked up for unjust reasons (Frankl, *Man's Search for Meaning*). He notes that in cases like the one faced by John the Baptist, prison tends to tear a person down and break the will of an individual. Frankl, a noted psychologist, found that for those who made it through such horror, simple survival was not their primary goal; they had to search for a meaning, find a purpose, in order to survive.

It is in such a situation that we find John. He's a captive, imprisoned unjustly, and he seeks to understand the meaning of his life. John's purpose had been to prepare the way for a "coming one"; he had been the herald, the announcer of the coming Messiah. And what a coming it was going to be, for John expected the messiah to be a fiery reformer who was going to separate the wheat from the chaff and cut down anything that did not bear good fruit (Luke 3:8–9). This fiery reformer was to come in power and might, and would conquer the worldly powers. Even the forceful John himself would be unworthy to undo the Messiah's sandals.

And so we find John sitting in prison and receiving reports about the activities of Jesus, wondering if Jesus is really the one. In response to the reports that he has received, John sends messengers to Jesus and they ask: "Are you the one who is to come, or should we expect another?" Jesus was not meeting John's expectations and was not living up to John's understanding of a "messiah." He was not acting like a fiery reformer or king coming in power. So the question emerges for John, and finally he sends disciples to find out the truth about this Jesus: "Are you the one who is to come?" (Luke 7:19). Once again, Luke has put a big pawprint on the page calling our attention to a story that answers John's probing question.

The disciples come and repeat verbatim John's question to Jesus, "Are you the one who is to come, or are we to wait for another?" This is a simple yes or no question—either Jesus is or he is not. So, we expect a simple answer. Yet the answer is not as simple as we might think, because Jesus does not respond in a straightforward manner. Instead, he just goes about his business and brings the two disciples of John along with him, so they can see what he is doing and who he is. He heals, he restores sight, he casts out evil spirits—in short, he fulfills the words that he had spoken to his hometown folks (Luke 4:18–19). Jesus has become the embodied promise of God, fulfilling God's salvific plans for the world.

The truth is this: Jesus just goes about being Jesus. He takes notice of the outcast, the downtrodden, the sick, and he works to heal, lift up, and impact their lives. Jesus takes John's disciples on an adventure with him, so that they encounter a person and a live presence instead of a simple spoken answer. As readers of the narrative, we too are invited along on the journey to encounter the Christ in action. For John's question is often our question, "Are you really the one?" In the midst of the prisons of our lives—illness, job loss, strife with friends and family, moves to nursing homes—we too are searching for meaning and asking questions.

Luke suggests that the answers come in the form of witnesses who testify to their experience of the presence and power of Jesus to embody God's promissory grace. After they have witnessed his work, Jesus sends John's disciples back with the message: "Go, tell John what you have seen and heard: the blind see, the lame walk, the lepers are clean, the deaf hear, the dead live, and the poor receive good news." John's disciples become witnesses to the power of the gospel. John and his disciples, however, had expected Jesus to be a fiery reformer, one who would act boldly in power and might to establish a kingdom. Needless to say, a Jesus who consorted with sinners, healed lepers, and gave good news to the poor was not their conception of the "coming one." They had expected one thing and found another. Yet now they were witnesses to the salvation of God at work in the world in an unexpected way.

Somehow, Jesus knew that he had not met their expectations, and by implication *our* expectations. Somehow, he knew that who he was and who John wanted him to be were not one and the same. So, he also gave John's disciples a blessing to carry back to John, "Blessed is anyone who takes no offense at me," or "Blessed is anyone who is not scandalized by who I really am." Just as with the townspeople, just as with the Pharisees, now John had encountered Jesus, and the box that John had built for Jesus has been burst and the walls torn down. Jesus was more than John expected. He did not neatly fit into the categories of those who encountered him. He was always someone more, someone who called for more from those he encountered. More than Joseph's son, he was the fulfillment of prophecies. More than a master rabbi, he had the authority of God. More than a fiery reformer, he brought reform by healing, caring, and bringing good news to the down and

---

What did people expect from a Messiah?

In Jesus' time there was a complex mixture of understandings about who the Messiah would be and what he would do. There were two general schools of thought: (1) The Messiah would be a descendant of David and would rule brilliantly over a new Israel in a blessed era of peace; (2) The Messiah would be a Son of Man, an otherworldly being who coexisted with God and would return at the end of this age to pass judgment. The concept of a Messiah who would suffer was completely unknown to the contemporaries of Jesus.

out. Luke continues to provide clues to the identity of Jesus and the character of his ministry, a ministry that Jesus will call his followers to embrace.

"Who is this who even forgives sins?" (7:36–50)

Through the use of questions, Luke has been building anticipation within the audience about the nature and character of Jesus' ministry. Immediately following Jesus' rendezvous with John's disciples, he finds himself invited to the home of a Pharisee to enjoy a meal. Before moving on, it is important to note that the Pharisees of Jesus' time have often been denigrated and held up as "straw men" to be easily torn down in contrast to Jesus. Pharisees, although they were not priests, were the good religious people of Jesus' day, trying their best to live all day, every day under the rule of God. In essence, their rules and regulations were not pious pomposity or religious nit-picking, but legitimate attempts to be faithful to a God who they believed provided order and direction for life and called God's chosen to a life of obedience. In fact, as Fred Craddock notes, "One does not have to strain to find much in common between Jesus and the Pharisees" (Craddock, 75).

Having been invited to Simon the Pharisee's house, Jesus encounters not only the Pharisee but a woman who was a "sinner," perhaps a prostitute, who wet his feet with tears, kissed them, and anointed them. Duly concerned and troubled by Jesus' lack of recognition of the "state" of the woman, the Pharisee opines within his heart that Jesus surely must not be a prophet, for "real" prophets do not consort with women of ill repute. In the face of the Pharisee's incredulity, Jesus tells a parable about forgiveness and the relationship of love and thankfulness: those who are forgiven much love much, while those who are forgiven little love little. "Here are two religious leaders suddenly in the presence of a sinful woman. One has an understanding of righteousness which causes him to distance himself from her; the other understands righteousness to mean moving toward her with forgiveness and a blessing of peace" (Craddock, 105).

Yet, as earlier with Zechariah the priest who disbelieves Gabriel and the young woman Mary who believes (Luke 1), the story is also about the contrast between how Simon the Pharisee and the sinful woman greet and understand their visitor, Jesus (Luke 7:44–46). She meets Jesus with the appropriate etiquette of hospitality, with washing of the feet, a kiss of greeting, and an anointing. She, the fallen one, has understood who this is, while the Pharisee has not. Jesus, the invited guest, is more than just a dinner guest; he is one who has the authority to forgive sins and evoke the love of the forgiven sinner (Luke 7:47–49). When Jesus utters words of forgiveness, however, the murmurs begin again and we encounter once more the pawprint on the page telling us to pay attention: "Who is this who forgives sins?" The question has been answered by the actions of the woman who greets Jesus with the hospitality of love, so that the Pharisee is confronted with an extraordinary dinner guest. Here again, the question "Who is this?" has exploded the expectations of those encountering Jesus, except for those like the woman in this story who receive forgiveness and are sent forth in peace (Luke 7:50).

"Who then is this?" (8:22–25)

Up until this point in the narrative, the disciples have not been the ones raising questions about the identity of Jesus. Instead, it has been his hometown folks, the Pharisees, and John and his followers. Unlike Mark, who portrays the disciples as little more than bumblers who are constantly confused by Jesus, Luke portrays the disciples as understanding and diligent followers, for they will later be the foundation for the gospel's spreading abroad as told by Luke in the sequel to the Gospel, the Acts of the Apostles. Yet here Jesus is alone with his disciples aboard a boat on the Sea of Galilee. There are echoes of the story of Jonah as Jesus falls asleep in the ship and a great storm arises (Luke 8:23). Like the sailors who confront Jonah, the disciples fear for their lives in the face of the tempest and wake Jesus. Jesus exorcises the storm and removes the danger (see Craddock, 114), so that the disciples marvel and muse, "Who then is this, that he commands even the winds and the water, and they obey him?" (Luke 8:25). Once again,

"Perhaps this accounts for some of his popularity: that a Messiah is coming is always an exciting and welcome message. Everyone had a sermon under the title 'When the Messiah Comes,' a message including every hope, every dream, every ideal condition for which the heart longs. It is no wonder that the church's message that the Messiah has come and he is Jesus has not been as popular. To believe the Messiah *has* come means we can no longer shape him to fit our dreams; he shapes us to fit God's will."—Fred B. Craddock, *Luke*, Interpretation, 127.

Luke has placed a pawprint on the page and we are encouraged to pay attention.

Even though they have been with him, the disciples still do not understand who the man is that lies asleep in their boat. After calming the storm, Jesus turns to the disciples and poignantly asks, "Where is your faith?" By this question Jesus seems to be "addressing their fear during the storm—fear, not doubt, being the opposite of faith. They had been with Jesus long enough to have adequate ground for trust in God and in Jesus' access to God's power" (Craddock, 115). And yet they feared. As in earlier scenes when someone asks the question "Who is this?" the disciples have expectations that are overturned, and Jesus is more than they have anticipated. This, however, is the first time that the question of identity has been raised in the inner circle, which points to the future confrontation where the question of "who" is placed on the lips of Jesus himself.

"Who is this about whom I hear such things?" (9:7–9)

His hometown people, the Pharisees, John, and now the disciples have noticed that someone unexpected and amazing has walked across the spectrum of history. Given all this recognition, it is not long before the political figurehead of the time, Herod, also takes notice of Jesus. In a description that foreshadows Jesus' later questioning of the disciples, Herod hears reports from the people that John is back, or perhaps Elijah or one like the prophets of old. These reports are disconcerting to a ruler who believed that he had solved his "religious fanatic problem" by the beheading of John. Now Jesus has come onto the radar screen of not only the religious leaders but the political leaders as well, for any suggestions that linked Jesus "to ancient prophecies about God's future for Israel could become socially and politically inflammatory" (Craddock, 123).

Once again, Luke has placed a pawprint on the page and called us to look closely at a clue. The identity of this one called Jesus will disturb not only the religious leaders of the day but also the political leaders, both of whom will later band together to rid themselves of this nuisance of a man (Luke 23). Herod's desire to meet Jesus foreshadows his later encounter with Jesus, where Jesus will eventually meet a fate like that of his cousin John—death.

"Who do you say that I am?" (9:18–22)

In the narrative, Jesus asks this question of his disciples, but clearly the narrative progression of clues within the text suggests that Luke intends this question to confront disciples of every age. The scene begins with Jesus at prayer, a signal we noted earlier that marks a significant moment in Luke's narrative. What follows is a second reporting of the popular opinions on the public square concerning Jesus: "Who do the people say that I am?" Echoing the reports given earlier to Herod, the disciples inform Jesus that the court of public opinion holds that he is the precursor of the messiah who is to come. The age is yet to come, and the messiah is on the horizon, and Jesus is but the herald, which means that the future still is held in abeyance and remains open.

> "He said to them, 'But who do you say that I am?' Peter answered, 'The Messiah of God.'"—Luke 9:20

> Perhaps this accounts for some of his popularity: that a Messiah is coming is always an exciting and welcome message. Everyone had a sermon under the title "When the Messiah Comes," a message including every hope, every dream, every ideal condition for which the heart longs. It is no wonder that the church's message that the Messiah has come and he is Jesus has not been as popular. To believe the Messiah *has* come means we can no longer shape him to fit our dreams; he shapes us to fit God's will. (Craddock, 127)

Following the recital of public opinion, Jesus turns the spotlight on the disciples and asks point-blank: "But who do you say that I am?" Given the directness of the question, this becomes the clearest pawprint that we have seen in Luke's Gospel up until this point. Peter answers for all those who have been examining the clues by proclaiming: "The Messiah of God." It is important to note that the specific response of Peter to Jesus' question varies from Gospel to Gospel (see Matt. 16:16 and Mark 8:29), as here in Luke Jesus is once again directly linked to God and God's structure of salvation. He is the one anticipated by Mary and rejoiced over by the angels, the one promised in the prophecies of Isaiah, the embodied presence of God's saving grace. Yet that embodied grace is also linked to the suffering Messiah, as Jesus connects his identity directly to a prediction of his passion. Luke does not record, as do Matthew and Mark, Peter's rejection of Jesus' suffering identity. Yet Luke provides his readers with a

38

quotation, unlike Matthew and Mark, of Jesus' request to the disciples to keep quiet about his identity, which is linked to his future trials and death.

Step by step and point by point, Luke has built his case for the identity of Jesus. He has baited the sleuths within his audience with all the appropriate clues, so that it has become clear who Jesus is. This clarity sets the stage for Jesus' future story and teaching, for now that we know who Jesus is, the question turns to us: who are we to be, who follow him? It is worth noting that the passage following the crescendo that has built within the audience, Luke 9:23–27, lays out the parameters of discipleship for those who would be bold enough to follow Jesus.

It seems that every Christmas, a few intrepid souls want to combat the commercialism of the season by bringing out the slogan "Jesus—He is the reason for the season." As Luke tells the story, Jesus is the reason that his followers have hope. We worship, we study, and we probe because we have met him long ago or we have heard about him and want to know more. We are searching for clues about who he is, because we want to know more about who we as Christians should be. Every time we find a clue about Jesus, every time we encounter him—just like the townspeople, the Pharisees, and even John the Baptist—we find that we have come with a box that Jesus must fit in, and he breaks the box. He is more than we expected and his "more" is not easily contained, but it is a more that calls us to costly obedience, a more that calls us not to be scandalized by one who ate and drank with sinners, a more that offers hope for those down-and-out moments of our lives. God does not leave us to blindly grope around, but gives us clues about the central character of our lives as Christians—Jesus.

> ## Want to Know More?
>
> **About Pharisees?** See *The New Westminster Dictionary of the Bible* (Philadelphia: Westminster Press, 1970), 741–42.
>
> **About Herod?** See *The New Westminster Dictionary of the Bible*, 379–84.
>
> **About messianic expectations?** See Celia Brewer Marshall, *A Guide through the New Testament* (Louisville, Ky.: Westminster John Knox Press, 1994), 33.

Questions for Reflection

1. What clues do we seek to help us know Jesus? How are these the same as or different from the clues sought by Jesus' contemporaries?

2. Jesus was asked to show his "spiritual ID" many times, as these passages show. Are you ever asked to show your spiritual ID? How do you answer?

3. Fred Craddock writes that "to believe the Messiah *has* come means we can no longer shape him to fit our dreams; he shapes us to fit God's will." How have we as a church tried to shape Jesus to fit our dreams? Why do we sometimes resist his efforts to shape us?

4. If Jesus asked you, how would you answer the question "Who do you say that I am?"

Journey to Jerusalem:
The Call to Discipleship

Perhaps they were sharing stories about what they had done the night before or what they were looking forward to in the days ahead. According to the news reports, she had just picked him up and they were heading home when it happened. They hit black ice. The car spun out of control, crashed, and flipped. The woman was knocked unconscious, but the four-year-old child in the car was not severely hurt, and thus began a story that made the national news a few years ago. This four-year-old boy, who himself received 24 stitches on his forehead, who thought that the unconscious woman, his mom, was dead, who was in the middle of nowhere in the dark of the early morning, crawled out of the car and set off. He set his face toward a point that he knew and walked a half mile down a dark street, apparently never veering too far to the left or to the right. He walked until he came to a house, knocked on the door and said: "The car crashed. My mommy's dead."

It is difficult to imagine what that walk must have been like. We find our minds questioning and wondering about a cold, dark street and a determined little boy. In the middle of the night and after a harrowing collision he had set his face to go down a dark and difficult road toward a goal that only he knew. He set his face, made up his mind, and in so doing ended up saving the life of his mother.

Setting the face—it's an idiom for determination, making up one's mind. It conjures an image of steely eyes looking down a difficult path with recognition of what lies ahead, but with the tenacity to make it down the way no matter what happens; or of a clenched jaw that cannot be deterred from its chosen path; or of a quiet persistence that will doggedly pursue its purpose until it has completed the task.

This concept of setting the face has a history in the Bible, as the suffering servant says in Isaiah, "I have set my face like flint, and I know that I shall not be put to shame" (Isa. 50:7; see also 2 Kings 12:17; Ezek. 6:2; 13:17). In each of these cases, we find that setting the face portends determination and at times a simple, yet firm, allegiance to the designs and purposes of God.

"He set his face . . ." (9:51)

Although the phrase appears rather innocuous and could be easily overlooked, for Luke it signals a dramatic turning point in the story of Jesus. While all the Gospels report Jesus' climactic trip to Jerusalem that eventually leads to his execution, Luke spends a large part of his Gospel with Jesus along the way. In fact, almost ten full chapters of Luke's Gospel are devoted to this journey (Luke 9:51–19:28) while the material associated with the final journey in Mark (Mark 10:1–52) and Matthew (chaps. 19–20) is comparatively sparse.

For Luke this is not a travelogue reporting precise details of movement toward Jerusalem from Galilee; nor is it a detailed itinerary that later followers of Jesus could use to retrace his footsteps in pilgrimages. In fact, reading through the pages one finds it difficult to trace Jesus' journey. Given the place-names and descriptions, it seems to be a meandering journey rather than one described by the phrase "setting the face," which as we have seen suggests dogged determination to journey directly toward the goal (see, e.g., Luke 9:51–53; 10:38ff.; 17:11). In light of this meandering, it would seem that some other purpose lies behind Luke's extended narrative of journey and his placement of the material within this section of his Gospel.

Without hazarding a trip into Luke's mind, the content and context of the material immediately prior to the pronouncement of Luke 9:51 and the passages within the travel narrative are at least suggestive for a creative understanding of this material. There we saw that a primary concern of the Gospel was to lay out the identity of the one called Jesus. Following the series of identity questions that were looked at in the last chapter, Jesus finally turned directly to his disciples and asked, "But who do you say that I am?" (Luke 9:20). Peter's reply, "The Messiah of God," functions doubly within the story—within the narrative as the response of those closest to Jesus during his ministry, and within the Gospel as the answer of those, like Theophilus, who desire to know the truth about the one who fulfills

God's promises (Luke 1:1–4). Through his narrative art, Luke has encouraged the readers of his text to join Peter in the proclamation of Jesus' true identity.

If faith were as easy as figuring out who Jesus is, the Gospel story could have ended with Peter's utterance. But there is more to the story than simply answering the question of Jesus' identity correctly. Jesus calls for disciples to follow him and to become like him, so that in coming to know the identity of Jesus, those who follow him come to understand who they are to be. This concept is as old as the first chapter of Genesis, which boldly states that human beings are created in the image of God (Gen. 1:26–28). Of all the pieces of Creation that God could have chosen to reflect the divine image on earth, God takes the gamble of placing the image within humanity. John Calvin, a key leader in the Protestant Reformation, began his magnum opus explicating the fundamentals of the Christian faith, *Institutes of the Christian Religion*, with a fairly simple premise: the more we learn about God, the more we learn about ourselves, and the more we learn about

> "Nearly all the wisdom we possess, that is to say, true and sound wisdom, consists of two parts: the knowledge of God and of ourselves. . . . Again, it is certain that man never achieves a clear knowledge of himself unless he has first looked upon God's face, and then descends from contemplating him to scrutinize himself."—John Calvin, *Institutes of the Christian Religion*, Library of Christian Classics, vol. 1 (Philadelphia: Westminster Press, 1960), 35, 37.

ourselves, the more we learn about God (Calvin, 1.1.1). In other words, we are who we represent, and the more we learn about God, the more we learn who we are to be. Following the same premise, Jesus now centers his ministry on informing his retinue of the nature of their identity as the ones who claim to emulate him; that is, in the material that follows Jesus' setting his face to go to Jerusalem, we find out what it means to be persons who will later bear the name of Jesus—Christians.

"... but they did not receive him" (9:52–55)

Immediately after Luke informs his audience that Jesus has set his face toward Jerusalem, the nature of the reception that Jesus will receive is spelled out in an encounter with the Samaritan villages. The relationship between the Jews and the Samaritans eroded over the years of history following the destruction of Israel in 721 B.C.E. by the Assyrians (see 2 Kings 17:5–41). Through a series of recriminations and arguments over the "true" bearers of the Hebrew tradition, an intrafamily gap had developed between these religious communities that could be described as hostile (e.g., the Samaritan opposition to the rebuilding of the Jerusalem wall and Temple in Nehemiah 4 and 6). It is in this "hostile" territory that Jesus begins the journey that will eventually find its culmination in Jerusalem. Luke will have further commentary on the Samaritans, especially since their animosity with the Jewish community means that they are seen as "outsiders," people seemingly beyond the bounds of the promised, covenant community.

In this context the Samaritans parallel the hometown people that Jesus encountered at the beginning of his Galilean ministry (Luke 4:16ff.). As Jesus began the earlier phase of his ministry, his hometown people rejected him and even sought his death, thus foreshadowing the coming rejection and death of Jesus. Similarly, as Jesus starts the new phase of his ministry characterized by the setting of his face toward Jerusalem, he confronts rejection. The Samaritan towns refuse to receive Jesus and those accompanying him, highlighting again the rejection that Jesus will endure throughout his earthly ministry as described by Luke.

The rejection by the Samaritans peals like a bell, sending forth alarm about impending danger. Jesus will not be received with open arms by the world that he has entered, but ultimately will be tried for sedition, deserted by his closest colleagues, and executed like a common criminal. "He came to what was his own, but his own people did not accept him" (John 1:11). The path upon which Jesus treads does not offer rose gardens and tea parties, but cost and burden. Abruptly and poignantly, Luke places the cards on the table about the nature of existence for those who follow Jesus—they will suffer rejection and rebuff.

Being rejected by the Samaritans, however, inspires anger and the lust for action in John and James. Perhaps incredulous at and incensed by the Samaritans' slight, they propose to call down fire to consume and destroy those who would offend their master. Jesus, on the other hand, follows his own directives, which he gave when he first sent the disciples to minister in the world (Luke 9:1–6). He

> "As we embark upon discipleship we surrender ourselves to Christ in union with his death—we give over our lives to death. Thus it begins; the cross is not the terrible end to an otherwise god-fearing and happy life, but it meets us at the beginning of our communion with Christ. When Christ calls a man, he bids him come and die."—Dietrich Bonhoeffer, *The Cost of Discipleship* (New York: Macmillan & Co., 1960), 79.

passes on by and does not return destruction upon the Samaritans for their lack of hospitality. Moreover, he rebukes John and James for their desire for destruction.

The course of the ministry has been set. Along that pathway Jesus will meet rejection and finally the ultimate rejection culminating in his death. It is a difficult path, but a path that all who claim the name Christian have also been called to follow. Luke's Gospel leaves no illusions about the costliness of following Jesus and does not tiptoe around the true nature of discipleship. Dietrich Bonhoeffer, a German theologian of the early twentieth century who was imprisoned by the Nazis, wrote a treatise called *The Cost of Discipleship*. Within the pages of that book, Bonhoeffer states: "When Christ calls a man, he bids him come and die" (Bonhoeffer, 99).

"I will follow you wherever you go" (9:57–62)

In his commentary on Luke, Fred Craddock precisely states the significance of this passage, which falls on the heels of Jesus' rejection by the Samaritans: "Had Jesus' words 'Take up your cross daily' never been spelled out concretely, they could have remained an ethereal ideal having the effect of background organ music or they could have sunk to some meaningless act of self-inflicted pain such as walking to work during Lent with a tack in one's shoe. Here, however, his words are translated into specific circumstances" (Craddock, 143). In the three vignettes that form the heart of this brief passage, the key question revolves around this cost of discipleship. By placing these brief encounters in this context, however, Luke has concretized faith so that it is not merely an assent to the nature of Jesus and his ministry, but an action plan that calls forth a particular type of response from its adherents. Each of the people who encounter Jesus in these five verses confronts head-on the call to "follow" and the difficult consequences of this confrontation.

Interpretations of these confrontations have often tried to water down the harshness of Jesus' demands in order to make them more palatable for modern sensitivities. The concern is that Jesus has laid too hard a task before those who would follow him, and that such a call would be too difficult to follow. Thus, there have been attempts to spiritualize and internalize the encounters so that the plain sense of the words can be ameliorated and the move to discipleship can become an internal assent without any external change of behavior or cost. These texts from Luke, however, will not allow Jesus to be discounted, candy-coated, and made more comfortable.

In the first encounter, a man comes to Jesus and proclaims: "I will follow you wherever you go" (Luke 9:57), an apparent declaration of willingness to go along the path that Jesus is traveling. The reply of Jesus, however, ups the ante and lays out for this would-be disciple the cost of following: "Foxes have holes, and birds of the air have nests; but the Son of Man has nowhere to lay his head" (Luke 9:58). The response of Jesus is not a simple call to win a lot of converts, but an honest declaration of the difficulties involved in the trek that he has assumed. It is as if Jesus has said to this would-be follower, "I am totally dependent on the hospitality of others; are you willing to be?" (Craddock, 144). Following the one who has set his face to Jerusalem does not promise ease and comfort, but dependence and trust on the generosity of others. Later on, Jesus will remind his followers of the providential care of God (Luke 12:22ff.), but those who accompany him must relinquish the need to manage and control, and simply trust.

> "The radicality of Jesus' words lies in his claim to priority over the best, not the worst, of human relationships. Jesus never said to choose him over the devil but to choose him over the family. And the remarkable thing is that those who have done so have been freed from possession and worship of family and have found the distance necessary to love them."—Fred B. Craddock, *Luke,* Interpretation, 144.

After the initial meeting, Jesus happens upon another and offers an appeal to this new person, "Follow me" (Luke 9:59). In response to Jesus' offer the individual appears to make a legitimate request, "Lord, first let me go and bury my father" (Luke 9:59). For the people of Jesus' society, filial obligations to one's parents overrode all other obligations, so that even a priest, normally prevented from all contact with dead bodies, could attend to the burial of his mother or father (Lev. 21:1–3). Throughout the early stories of Genesis, one of the constant motifs is the gathering of the sons, even those who had been estranged from one another, to bury their father (see Isaac and Ishmael in Gen. 25:9; Esau and Jacob in Gen. 35:29; and Joseph and his brothers in Gen. 50:7). Within this context, the request of the individual seems perfectly reasonable, but Jesus replies: "Let the dead bury their own dead; but as for you, go and proclaim the kingdom of God" (Luke 9:60). This amazingly harsh statement demonstrates that no loyalty or obligation supersedes the obligation to Jesus. Again, the cost of following is high.

Finally, one more person approaches Jesus and calls out: "I will follow you, Lord; but let me first say farewell to those at my home"

(Luke 9:61). The maker of this request has good biblical precedent for this petition, as the Old Testament prophet Elisha had been granted permission to return home and say farewell to his parents when Elijah had placed the call of God upon Elisha's life (1 Kings 19:20ff.). Once again, however, Jesus sets his cards firmly on the table and reveals the implications of his call: "No one who puts a hand to the plow and looks back is fit for the kingdom of God" (Luke 9:62).

> "The point Jesus was making is that in everything there is a crucial moment; if that moment is missed the thing most likely will never be done at all. The man in the story had stirrings in his heart to get out of his spiritually dead surroundings; if he missed that moment he would never get out."—William Barclay, *The Gospel of Luke,* rev. ed., Daily Study Bible, 132.

The replies of Jesus to these possible converts must have stopped his disciples in their tracks; they continue to do so today. For those who would want to market Jesus, his responses in Luke 9 will not make an easy pitch possible, and indeed might drive them crazy. Every time a prospect enters the door, Jesus keeps upping the ante, making it harder to follow him, and laying his cards right out on the table about the difficulty of being his disciple. The call to follow is not as light as it may appear.

Each year Christians celebrate Ash Wednesday as the beginning of the Lenten season, a season in which we focus on the life of Christ that has been offered for us. Each year, as we concentrate on what Jesus has given up for us, many people offer to give up chocolate, dairy products, or some other part of their daily lives as a symbol of their understanding of the gift that Jesus has made in his life, death, and resurrection. While these relinquishments may serve a symbolic purpose, Luke claims that following Jesus is no trivial matter and should not be taken lightly. Luke reminds us not to kid ourselves about what it means to be a

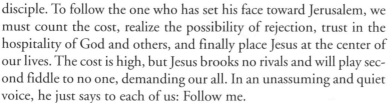

Want to Know More?

About Lent? See J. G. Davies, ed., *The New Westminster Dictionary of Liturgy and Worship* (Philadelphia: Westminster Press, 1986), 299–300.

About the Samaritans? See Paul J. Achtemeier, ed., *HarperCollins Bible Dictionary,* rev. ed. (San Francisco: Harper-SanFrancisco, 1996), 963–66.

disciple. To follow the one who has set his face toward Jerusalem, we must count the cost, realize the possibility of rejection, trust in the hospitality of God and others, and finally place Jesus at the center of our lives. The cost is high, but Jesus brooks no rivals and will play second fiddle to no one, demanding our all. In an unassuming and quiet voice, he just says to each of us: Follow me.

Questions for Reflection

1. John Calvin wrote that the more we learn about God, the more we learn about ourselves, and the more we learn about ourselves, the more we learn about God. How can learning about God teach us about ourselves? How can learning about ourselves teach us about God?

2. Jesus set his face and was unwavering in his goal. Have you ever "set your face" toward an important destination? Are there dangers in setting your face?

3. In this passage one man asks to go home to bury his father before he follows Jesus. Jesus replies, "Let the dead bury their own dead; but as for you, go and proclaim the kingdom of God" (Luke 9:60). Another man wishes to bid his family farewell, but Jesus replies, "No one who puts a hand to the plow and looks back is fit for the kingdom of God." Why does Jesus make it so hard to follow him?

4. Have you ever given an answer like the ones in this passage to a request to follow Jesus? What were the results?

5

The Good Samaritan: A Way of Life

In many ways biblical phrases and images have seeped into our culture and our language. One phrase that has come to be part of ordinary conversation and part of the milieu at large is "good Samaritan." It seems that people who risk their lives in rescue situations receive the title "good Samaritan." The young man who helps change the flat tire on the retired couple's car in the middle of the night receives the adulation of the couple: "Thanks for being our good Samaritan." The person who intervenes on behalf of the child in the face of bullies receives thanks from the parents: "Thank you for watching out for my child and being his good Samaritan." The medical person who witnesses a terrible traffic accident and goes to the aid of the victims is called a good Samaritan in the morning newspapers. In fact, many states have so-called "Good Samaritan" laws on their books to protect from lawsuits those who offer aid to accident victims, encouraging those who are medically trained to intervene without fear of repercussion.

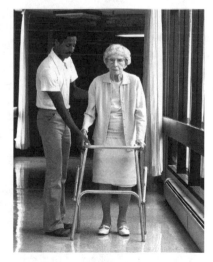

Without denying the significance of this usage and the good that has been done for people under the auspices of the term *good Samaritan,* confronting the text in Luke 10:25–37 raises questions about understanding the parable as only a morality play—a story that can be boiled down to a simple sentence that can then be applied as a moral for life. While on the surface it may not appear to be all that bad to use the term *good Samaritan* in instances of heroism and bravery, this usage can have a tendency to water down the parable Jesus told to the simple statement: "Do good for other people." It is true that this is a worthy goal and statement about life, but if this is all we take away from the story, then the text and the encounter with Jesus become secondary and almost the dross that can be discarded once the meaning has been refined. If Jesus had only desired to have people "do good," why tell this particular story instead of stating a bold imperative? Is there a reason that the story is about a Samaritan and not a disciple, Jew, or Roman? What function do the three encounters with a beaten man have within the text? Without minimizing the significance of doing good for others, let us look at whether there is something more to this story told by Jesus on the way to Jerusalem.

The First Questions (10:25–29)

As noted in the previous chapter, the context for the encounter described in these verses is Jesus' journey to Jerusalem. Luke has moved into the point of his description of the life of Jesus where he focuses on the nature of discipleship as Jesus has set his face to go to Jerusalem. Along this journey, the disciples are being incorporated and indoctrinated into the truth regarding the character of their discipleship. At this point in the narrative, Jesus has commissioned more than twelve to carry forth his message (Luke 10:1ff.). These disciples have returned from their missionary journeys and are reporting back to Jesus the results of their activities (Luke 10:17), so that Jesus rejoices and proclaims to them privately that they have been given the privilege of seeing and hearing marvels that prophets and kings had desired to see but never did (Luke 10:23–24). It is at this moment that they are interrupted by a lawyer who asks a question of Jesus. Through the use of "just then" in 10:25, Luke has limited the audience of this engagement to the disciples, which suggests that Jesus has directed his words not only at the lawyer, but specifically at those who have chosen to follow him. The stage is set for a private teaching for those on the inside about the character of their obedience along the path.

While Luke does not provide the reader with a detailed description of the reasons behind the lawyer's action, he notes that the question that has been offered is not one of friendly inquiry. The lawyer arose and asked his question in order to put Jesus to the test. Throughout Luke's Gospel, lawyers, who were charged in Jewish society with the administration and comprehension of the law, are pictured in a negative light (see 7:30, 11:45, 46, 52; 14:3) and this lawyer is no different. In fact, the only other mention of "testing" in Luke's Gospel is the quotation of Deuteronomy 6:16 in Luke 4:12, where Jesus finishes his duel with the devil by stating firmly that one should not "test" the Lord God. By framing the introduction of the lawyer in this way, Luke has prepared the reader to pay attention, as something more than a cordial conversation is about to happen.

> "Jesus has said the wise and prudent miss what babes understand. This story illustrates the truth of that word."—Fred B. Craddock, *Luke,* Interpretation, 149.

The lawyer frames his inquiry around the question of eternal life and daily living requirements. By responding to the lawyer's question with another question, Jesus forces the lawyer to answer his own test (Luke 10:26). Jesus engages in the dialogue along a typical Jewish and rabbinic line of thought, as he encourages his questioner to seek the answer in the law, the Torah. A contemporary of Jesus, the rabbi Hillel, once stated that the one "who has gained for [himself or herself] the words of the Torah has gained . . . the life of the world to come" (Hillel as quoted in Bailey, *Through Peasant Eyes,* 36). The lawyer responds by combining two texts, one from Deuteronomy 6:5 and the other from Leviticus 19:18, into an answer to the question "What are the primary and uttermost understandings of the law?" (See Matt. 22:37–40 and Mark 12:29–31). It is interesting to note that throughout the Old and New Testaments, the relationship between devotion to God and the treatment of the neighbor are intertwined (e.g., the first four commandments, which focus on the vertical relationship, and the last six, which focus on interactions with other human beings: Exodus 20 and Deuteronomy 5; see also Hos. 4:1–3; Micah 6:6–8; 1 John 4:7–12).

Following the recital of the two Old Testament texts, the lawyer is commended by Jesus and given a promise: "Do this, and you will live" (Luke 10:28). As we have seen earlier, throughout Luke's Gospel there has been an emphasis on hearing and obeying (see chap. 1), so that Jesus' response echoes the call for obedience—"You know what is required, now live it out." Given that Luke has prepared his audience for a confrontation, however, the lawyer's response comes as no surprise. Desiring to justify himself, the lawyer asks another question: "Who is my neighbor?" Shifting the focus, the lawyer seeks clarification and

51

a limitation on the earlier commandments by asking another question that moves away from simple obedience to detailed "theological" reflection; in other words, the lawyer has moved away from the imperative of action, "Do this," to a call for definition, "Who is." (See Brueggemann, *Genesis,* 48ff., for a further exploration of the move away from obedience to avoidance through theological reflection.)

The Parable of the Good Samaritan (10:30–35)

Immediately, Jesus engages the lawyer and the listening disciples with a story. Throughout the Gospels of Matthew, Mark, and Luke, Jesus is a teller of stories, and his stories often consist of parables. Parables have been defined in a variety of ways over the centuries—from an "earthly story with a heavenly meaning" to "a story that points beyond itself to a deeper truth." Parables, however, are more than stories that have a simple moral that once discovered can replace the parable, allowing it to be discarded. Parables invite their hearers to enter a new world created by the story in the imagination and to exist in that world for a while, so that one's own life and understanding of the world can then be compared to and critiqued by the imaginary world created by the parable. Parables invite us to picture and to live in a world different from our own, a world that usually calls into question our presuppositions and understandings about life. Much like the words of the prophets of ancient Israel, these words stoke our imaginations, inviting us to see anew the world in which we live. (On this understanding of the function of prophecy, see Brueggemann, *The Prophetic Imagination.*)

Jesus tells a story about a traveler going from Jerusalem to Jericho, a journey with which his hearers would have been familiar. The road from Jerusalem to Jericho, remnants of which can still be seen today in Israel, was a winding, narrow path that in many places did not allow the traveler to see farther than a few yards ahead on the journey. So it is not surprising that this road was known as a haven for thieves and robbers, and Jesus informs his audience that the lonely traveler has fallen into such hands. Beaten nearly to death and stripped of all possessions, the man is left half dead by the side of the road. While he is in this helpless situation, three visitors pass by and react to the man in different ways.

The story is often told and heard in our world so that the first two visitors are cast in an extremely negative light, as if Jesus is setting up straw men to easily knock over as the tale goes on. This negative characterization, however, finds no support in the parable. Fred Craddock notes: "First, painting unnecessarily unattractive portraits of the priest and Levite greatly weakens the story. The force of the parable depends very much on its realism and its ability to invite people to identify with characters within it. If the priest and Levite are presented as ethically dead and totally void of human caring, then no listener will say, 'I too behave that way'" (Craddock, 151).

As Luke tells his Gospel, priests and Levites are generally portrayed in a positive light and Jesus often shows respect for the office of the priest (e.g., Luke 1:5; 5:14; 17:14). Given this positive context, the reaction of the priest and the Levite to the situation may have been somewhat unexpected. No reasons are given for the fact that both men pass by, rather quickly, on the opposite side of the road from the fallen man; so making judgments on their character from the sparse amount of information given is difficult. One might suppose, however, that since there was a cultic prohibition regarding the touching of dead bodies—so that the one who came in contact with a dead body was ritually unclean, defiled, and unable to perform religious duties—the priest and Levite passed on by to avoid risking their jobs and livelihoods. Also, there was the possible danger that the man had been left there in order that the robbers might ambush the next passerby. These, however, are merely suppositions. The text does not provide clues into the motivations of the priest and Levite; it just describes their passing by on the other side.

While Jesus' audience may have been slightly surprised to see the religious leaders of the day passing by, the response of the third person happening by on the road provides the most shocking moment in the story. The third person is a Samaritan. In the previous chapter, we have seen that the enmity existing between the Samaritans and the Jews ran deep, so that Jesus' audience would have seen the Samaritan as the last possible person who would act compassionately. But that is exactly what happens, as the Samaritan acts just as quickly to assist the man beside the road as the priest and Levite had acted to pass by on the other side. The Samaritan has compassion, a characteristic only associated with Jesus, God, and the Prodigal's father in

> "Nobody would have dreamed of defining 'neighbor' to include Samaritans. . . . For him to . . . portray the Samaritan as the model of one who integrates love of God and love of neighbor, as the model whom true believers are to emulate, was outrageously shocking . . ."—Keith F. Nickle, *Preaching the Gospel of Luke* (Louisville, Ky.: Westminster John Knox Press, 2000), 123.

53

the rest of Luke's Gospel (Luke 1:78; 7:13; and 15:20), which further highlights the unexpected nature of his activity.

The reaction of the early hearers of this parable, given their prejudice toward Samaritans, would have been one of shock: This person does not know what compassion means! How dare he suggest that one of "them" could act with such care! Not only does the Samaritan offer care to the beaten victim, he binds his wounds, carries him to an inn, and provides for his stay, even promising to cover all the expenses incurred by the innkeeper in the care of the victim. Through his actions, the Samaritan reverses the activity of the bandits: the bandits took money, the Samaritan gave; the bandits beat, the Samaritan bound wounds; the bandits left for dead and did not return, the Samaritan left in absolute care and promised to return (Bailey, 73). With the promise of return and continued care, the parable ends, but not without challenging the audience about their prejudices concerning other people.

The Final Question (10:36–37)

Not only do the Samaritan's actions end the story, but Jesus calls his hearers back to the interpretive task by posing a question: "Which of these three, do you think, was a neighbor to the man . . . ?" (Luke 10:36). As with the first set of questions, Jesus has ultimately answered the question of the Pharisee with another question. Through the telling of the story and the rephrasing of the question, Jesus has changed the question from a limit-seeking question about the identity of the neighbor to a limitless question about acting neighborly. The Pharisee wanted to reflect and ponder the nature of the neighbor, so that it would be easy to say to whom one must act neighborly. Jesus, however, refuses the move away from obedience and action, focusing the spotlight on the actions of the Samaritan and summoning the lawyer to the bench for an answer.

> "Remember that this man who delayed his own journey, expended great energy, risked danger to himself, spent two days' wages with the assurance of more, and promised to follow up on his activity was ceremonially unclean, socially an outcast, and religiously a heretic. That is a profile not easily matched."—Fred B. Craddock, *Luke*, Interpretation, 151.

As the story ends, the lawyer answers Jesus' final question. Yet his answer still expresses shock and outrage at the story, as the lawyer cannot use the word Samaritan in his answer and only refers obliquely to the third passerby on that lonesome road between Jerusalem and Jericho. The Pharisee's answer, however, highlights two of the key emphases of Luke's Gospel—acting in obedience (i.e., doing; see above) and mercy, which is an action usually occurring in Luke with reference to the action of God (e.g., Luke 1:50, 54, 58, 72, 78). Later in Luke's Gospel the blind man beside the road asks Jesus to have mercy on him and Jesus will not pass him by, providing a living example of the Pharisee's final answer (Luke 18:35–42).

> "Whether we take the Samaritan as racially a Samaritan or as a heretic and a loose-liver branded with that name of contempt, the fact emerges that there may be more real Christianity in someone with a hot heart and a stained record than in someone who is coldly and correctly ortho-dox."—William Barclay, *The Parables of Jesus* (Louisville, Ky.: Westminster John Knox Press, 1999), 84.

The text ends with an imperative to "Go and do likewise." So, we find ourselves where we began. The story does call us to act as neighbors, but it also expands our concept of the neighbor. It is a call for "random acts of kindness," but it is more, as it overthrows our boundaries concerning whom we will offer kindness—"Love your enemies, do good to those who hate you" (Luke 6:27). The "good Samaritan" calls a people experiencing the journey with Jesus, the fulfillment of salvation (Luke 1:1–4), to a way of life involving neighborly love. In his sequel to the Gospel, the book of Acts, Luke reports that many of the activities of the early church reflect the ethic laid out in the "good Samaritan" story (Acts 4:32–5:11), while Peter's change in understanding with regard to the Roman outsider Cornelius demonstrates the overturning of assumptions and prejudices inherent in the parable of the good Samaritan (Acts 10:1–48).

Like the early church, in this parable we find at least an ethical call to action for those who will call themselves "Christians," followers of the one who has set his face toward Jerusalem. Yet as participants in that journey, we will also find our worldview changed, overturned, and rearranged

Want to Know More?

About the Good Samaritan and Christian ethics? See Paul Ramsey, *Basic Christian Ethics* (Louisville, Ky.: Westminster John Knox Press, 1993), 92–94.

About Parables? See Robert H. Stein, *An Introduction to the Parables of Jesus* (Philadelphia: Westminster Press, 1981), 27–35; James L. Bailey and Lyle D. Vander Broek, *Literary Forms in the New Testament: A Handbook* (Louisville, Ky.: Westminster John Knox Press, 1992), 105–14.

About the different types of Jewish religious leaders? See Alyce M. McKenzie, *Matthew,* Interpretation Bible Studies (Louisville, Ky.: Geneva Press, 1998), 3.

About the use of imagination for understanding biblical texts? See Walter Brueggemann, *The Prophetic Imagination* (Philadelphia: Fortress Press, 1978).

so that we will be forced to let go of any boundaries or limits on the idea of neighbor. Jesus' story continues to impact us today as do the questions: What boundaries have we placed on our love? Who are the people beaten, lying by the road, that we are passing by because we do not want to become unclean? Luke reminds us that the one posing these questions is Jesus, the one who walks down the road to Jerusalem, where he will be beaten and crucified to show the ultimate neighbor-love for us. Jesus calls us both to expand our worldview with regard to neighbors and to act on that expanded worldview. We are to act, empowered by the love of Christ seen in the cross, Christ who has accepted our beaten roadside bodies and challenged us to "Go and do likewise."

? Questions for Reflection

1. The parable of the good Samaritan is often viewed as a simple "morality play": Do good for other people. Think back to when you first heard the parable. What was its message to you then? How has that message changed?

2. The priest and the Levite are often portrayed almost as villains; yet this was probably not Jesus' intent. Why is it important that we not see these two men simply as uncaring travelers?

3. Who are the Samaritans in our world today? Who are the Samaritans in your life?

4. The scribe asked Jesus, "And who is my neighbor?" (Luke 10:29). Do you think he was satisfied with Jesus' answer? What *was* Jesus' answer?

The Dangers of Money

In his recent novel *The Testament,* John Grisham tells a story of greed, avarice, and the love of money. The story concerns the distribution of the estate of an eccentric, self-made billionaire, Troy Phelan, among his children. Phelan's legitimate, but estranged, children are all portrayed as corrupted by their desire for the riches to which they believe they are entitled following the death of their father. Yet there is an illegitimate daughter, Rachel Lane, who is a missionary in Brazil and to whom Phelan has left all his money. The plot turns around the machinations of those blinded by dollar signs and the extent to which they will go in order to seize fortune and power. In the midst of all the twists and turns, Grisham explores the greed of some of the characters, but also the disarming nonchalance of Rachel, who has discovered another reality through her work in the jungles of Brazil.

Money, and the love of it, is the primary subject and key plot line of countless novels, plays, and movies. Dozens of magazines are devoted to understanding and using it in the "best" manner possible. Infomercials air nightly on cable TV with new ideas about getting rich quick, while lotteries hold out the possibility of instant fortune. Money, how to make it and how to spend it, dominates the media in the "information age." Yet within the walls of Christian fellowship, we find a strange silence about money. In most churches, the topic of money remains taboo, to be discussed only on stewardship Sunday once a year and when a special need arises that requires a congregation's attention. "Among church members only *3 percent* say they ever discuss their finances with other church members. And only *4 percent* have ever discussed their finances with a member of the clergy" (Wuthnow, 141). It is a simple fact, however, that there are more references in the Bible to money and possessions than to any single subject other than God.

Beginning with Mary's song, moving along past the announcement to the shepherds (the lowest people on the economic scale) of the birth of a Savior, and continuing through Jesus' temptations and on into the rest of the Gospel, Luke is not silent about riches and the wealthy, along with poverty and the poor. For Luke, the gospel embodied in the person of Jesus speaks directly to questions about rich and poor, so much so that many see his Gospel as particularly concerned with those of lower economic status. Given that the journey narrative of Luke's Gospel (Luke 9:51–19:28) deals in part with outlining the life of discipleship, it is no surprise that Luke places many of Jesus' teachings concerning wealth and material possessions in this section of his narrative (besides the passages discussed here, see also Luke 11:39ff.; 16:1–13, 19–31; 18:18–30; 19:1–27). Many of the key themes of Luke's presentation can be found in the series of three interconnected passages occurring in Luke 12:13–21, 22–31, and 32–34. These passages have been described as follows: "Thus there appears to be a wide consensus that the passage at hand [12:22–34] contains the impossible admonitions of an idealistic Jesus who understands himself to be giving sound advice!" (Wheeler, 61). Given this description, these texts are often easily glossed over and dismissed as peripheral to the life of faith. On the other hand, as Wheeler and others have discovered, these passages are not the eccentric ramblings of a starry-eyed prophet, but central to understanding Jesus and the message of fulfillment he embodies.

The Rich Fool (12:13–21)

> "The ugly dispute is all too familiar: haggling over furniture, dishes, silverware, house, land, and savings account left by the deceased. Jesus is asked to be a referee and he refuses; after all, who can judge whose greed is right?"—Fred B. Craddock, *Luke,* Interpretation, 163.

Like Grisham's novel *The Testament,* this section in Luke begins with a dispute over an inheritance. Jesus has been speaking to the crowd about the significance of bold declarations (Luke 12:1–12) when someone from the crowd interrupts him, asking Jesus to settle a family dispute with regard to an inheritance. Jesus, ever the teacher, has seen into and beyond the man's question and moves the discussion to the heart of the issue: greed and the covetous desire to obtain property (see Ex. 20:17; Deut. 5:21; Mark 7:22; Rom. 1:29). As the characters and story line from *The Testament* indicate, this issue of greed and the lengths to which people will go to achieve prosperity remains as much an issue today as it was in Jesus' time.

After reminding his audience that life is more than abundant possessions (Luke 12:15), Jesus tells them an illustrative parable to further engage their imaginations regarding the danger of greed (Luke 12:16–21). Earlier, we saw that parables invite us into a different world so we can gain perspective on our own worldviews and critique them. Within this parable, we are invited into the world of a rich man whose crops have produced abundantly, perhaps indicating a significant blessing of God (Deut. 8:7–10; Ps. 1:1–3; Prov. 8:14–20). This rich man, who already has enough, now has been blessed with more than enough to meet his own needs. He has not gained his wealth through unjust means—extorting it from the poor or stealing from others—but has been blessed through a good harvest, wise use of his resources, and good investment in productive lands.

The parable raises the question about what to do with this "more than enough," and the man begins an inner dialogue. Most commentators on the passage see the descriptions of this inner dialogue as the crux of the parable, as the man "lives completely for himself, he talks to himself, he plans for himself, he congratulates himself" (Craddock, 163). The response of the man to his abundance is to try and secure it for himself, by tearing down barns that could not handle the overflow and building larger ones. He is completely satisfied with his actions, saying: "Soul, you have ample goods laid up for many years; relax, eat, drink, be merry" (Luke 12:19). Up until this point, the portrait of the rich man appears to be one of prudence and wise hedging against the future.

This portrait, however, becomes challenged by the intervention of God's perspective. Throughout the Old and New Testaments, human actions often appear to be autonomous and out of the purview of God, but God's engagement of the world changes the perception of the actions that have been undertaken. The prime example of this narrative move is in the David and Bathsheba story of 2 Samuel 11,

According to William Barclay, in his book *The Parables of Jesus* (Louisville, Ky.: Westminster John Knox Press, 1999, 121–26), the "Rich Fool" remembered the wrong things and forgot the right things. What he remembered: He remembered himself selfishly, and he remembered this world without a care for anything else. What he forgot: He forgot his neighbors; he forgot time, thinking his was unlimited; he forgot God; and he forgot that a man is what he is and not what he has.

where the whole narrative is told seemingly outside of God's vision, but ends with the bold declaration: "But the thing that David had done displeased the LORD" (2 Sam. 11:27b). In this parable, the only perspective available to the audience up to this point has been that of the rich man, who judges that his actions have been both prudent and wise to secure himself against the unknown future. The entrance of God in verse 20, however, immediately transforms this understanding.

God's first reaction is to declare, "You fool!" (Luke 12:20). The actions of the man are not evil, not wicked, not perverse. They are foolish because they lack perspective and wisdom: "Fools say in their hearts, 'There is no God'" (Ps. 14:1; 53:1). The self-absorbed, self-concerned, and self-fulfilled rich man has been acting as if he is autonomous, set apart from the rest of the world, and without care

"Do not forget the LORD your God."

or concern about other perspectives. The rich man has forgotten that God is the one who provides blessings, and has said to himself, "My power and the might of my own hand have gotten me this wealth" (Deut. 8:17). Jesus' parable does not inform us precisely that the rich man's abundance has caused him to forget God, but the ancient text of Deuteronomy 8 suggests that this indeed is the danger: prosperity will produce forgetfulness in those who experience it. They will forget the bigger picture of God and become solely interested in the self.

The next declaration of God further highlights the folly of the man's attitude, as the rich man's death that evening will foil all his future plans. Someone once asked one of the heirs of Aristotle Onassis's fortune, "How much did he leave behind?" The heir coolly responded, "Everything." Death, the eternal equalizer, shows the foolishness of the man's plans, as his grasping has no effect and all his plans become null and void. Following this change in the course of the story, Jesus ends with a wisdom statement: "So it is with those who store up treasures for themselves but are not rich toward God" (Luke 12:21). The rich man has tried to live his life apart from God;

he has tried to grasp security and grip it firmly; he has concentrated solely on himself and his own welfare. In the face of the anxiety of the future, he has tried to manipulate his own safety by storing treasures on earth, treasures that, as Jesus will inform us in a few verses, are fleeting when compared to the treasures provided by God.

"Do not worry" (12:22–32)

Up to this point, the audience for Jesus' teaching has been the entire crowd of people who have gathered around to listen. Now, however, Jesus turns to those who follow him closely, the disciples, and expounds further on their relationship to wealth and the riches of the world. By narrowing the focus of the ostensible audience, Luke has informed his readers that what follows is "insider information"; that is, the crowd may overhear his words, but these words are directed specifically at those who would follow after him.

The message that Jesus offers the disciples can be summed up in two words: "Don't worry." Far from being the genesis of the popular song "Don't Worry—Be Happy," Jesus' mandate to a lack of anxiety arises out of his conviction, developed deeply through his religious heritage, that God will provide for God's children (see, e.g., Gen. 22:8; Ex. 16:13–15; Deut. 8:3–4; Pss. 78:21–29; 104:27–30). Jesus' exhortation is based not on a Pollyanna view of the world that always looks on the bright side of life, but on the character and nature of a God who will not let go and who will provide (Rom. 8:31–39). Instead of acting like the rich fool who places his trust in his own machinations, Jesus encourages his disciples to trust in God alone.

> "The concerns here, however, like the retirement plan of the rich man, are concerns about future security. Such worries plague the well-to-do, while the very poor are concerned with immediate survival needs." Sharon H. Ringe, *Luke*, Westminster Bible Companion, 178.

Of course, this is easier said than done. As one pastor was leading a series of classes on faith and money, he asked the participants in the class to fill in the blank for two simple statements: "Money provides _____" and "Money does not provide _____." With each class of adults of different ages, the most frequent answers remained fairly constant throughout: "Money provides security" and "Money does not provide happiness." For most people, however, security and happiness are intertwined in such a way that a certain ambiguousness arises with regard to wealth: I think I need it to feel secure, but it won't provide me ultimate joy—so what do I do? "Everyone, of course, protests that he or she only wants enough, but no one knows how much is enough until one has too much" (Craddock, 163–64). In the face of this ambiguity, which produces a fixation on material possessions, Jesus answers simply: "Don't worry—Trust God." Jesus proposes three reasons why his disciples should not be anxious: "It [anxiety] is *inadequate* because it springs from an inadequate understanding of human life (v. 23); it is *unnecessary* because God who feeds the birds will feed them (v. 24); and it is *ineffective* because no one can add anything to his life by it (v. 25)" (Wheeler, 63).

In the midst of this claim on behalf of God's providence over and against anxiety, the most poignant imagery that Jesus uses originates from the realm of nature. Knowing that much of human anxiety focuses on food and clothing, Jesus centers his arguments on these concerns using the birds of the air and the lilies of the field as his lenses to focus the audience's attention. Luke, unlike Matthew and Mark, notes that Jesus describes the birds as ravens, unclean birds according to the Old Testament (Lev. 11:15; Deut. 14:14). This further highlights the example he is drawing, since he points out that God provides food even for unclean animals who neither plant nor sow. Similarly, he draws upon the image of lilies, which Isaiah 40:6–7 and other texts see as an image for the impermanence of life, noting that even lilies that will die tomorrow are far more beautifully clothed than Israel's most regal king, Solomon, ever was. Much like the psalmist in Psalm 8, Jesus calls attention to the created order and then proclaims the unique and special place of humanity in that order. God, who provides for the ravens and gives the lilies their beauty, can be trusted to take care of human beings, a unique part of God's created order.

In concluding this teaching on anxiety, Jesus makes three claims about God (Luke 12:30–32). First, God knows what human beings need. God is not uninvolved, unaware, and unconcerned, but intimately knows the needs of God's created beings. Second, God desires that human beings seek the kingdom of God; that is, God desires that we live under the auspices of the rule of God, not like the rich fool who tried to live his life as if God did not exist. (See the discussion of Luke 9:51–62 in unit 4; 10:25–37 in unit 5; and 14:1–24 in unit 7 for further discussion of the nature of kingdom living.) Finally, God delights to give the kingdom to God's children. God is a cheerful giver, who gives abundantly of grace and provision for living.

"Sell your possessions" (12:33–34)

The final two verses within this section of teaching presuppose the earlier teachings regarding the rich fool and anxiety. In the midst of a world where people take seriously the reality of God so that they do not grasp for security or live lives of unbridled anxiety, the commandment to sell and give makes sense. Trusting in God, disciples are able to provide for the needs of the poor and those less fortunate because they have been freed from the need to manipulate their own lives. The injunction to give alms and respond to the needs of the poor runs throughout the scriptures (Ex. 23:11; Deut. 15:7–11; Ps. 41:1; Isa. 58:7; Matt. 19:21; Rom. 15:26). Jesus goes on to say that despite appearances to the contrary, selling and giving are actually storing and collecting treasure. This time, however, the treasure being stored is imperishable in a purse that will not wear out and is secure from both theft and the ravages of time. Recalling the final words of the parable of the rich fool, Jesus now concretizes what it means to be rich toward God (Luke 12:21).

At the end of this section, Jesus provides a barometer for his disciples to measure their understanding of his teaching. A seemingly inoffensive statement about the location of one's treasure and heart becomes a measure of understanding, for the truth is: Where your treasure is, your heart will follow. The story is told about a pastor who preached a sermon that said the measure of your faith is what you give to your church. Within the congregation, some nodded yes and some were offended, but most knew at some deep level that the message hit on target. "It is striking that the churches timid and tentative on the subject of money have taught and preached the reverse of verse 34, making appeals for the listeners' hearts on the assumption that where the heart is, there the treasure will be. After reaping a harvest of hearts but very little support for the budget, some have come to acknowledge the realism of Jesus' words: where the possessions are, there the heart will be" (Craddock, 164).

Treasures, money, and wealth are not topics that roll off the tongue in most church situations. Where churches have been reluctant to address the issue of money, Jesus took on the topic as being one of the central struggles of people in their everyday lives. In addressing these issues, Jesus hits on the issue that lies beneath the surface—the issue of trust in the face of anxiety. We hear a lot today about scare tactics in the political arena, but much of the advertising that we encounter also works on the concept of fear: you're not safe, you're not young anymore, you're not having enough fun, you're not eating right, and so forth; buy this product to ensure safety, youth, fun, health, and on and on.

Dietrich Bonhoeffer wrote, "Earthly possessions dazzle our eyes and delude us into thinking that they can provide security and freedom from anxiety. Yet all the time they are the very source of all anxiety. If our hearts are set on them, our reward is an anxiety whose burden is intolerable. Anxiety creates its own treasures and they in turn beget further care. When we seek for security in possessions we are trying to drive out care with care, and the net result is the precise opposite of our anticipations. The fetters which bind us to our possessions prove to be cares themselves" (Bonhoeffer, 158).

Want to Know More?

About biblical views on money, possessions, and stewardship? See William R. Phillippe, *A Stewardship Scrapbook* (Louisville, Ky.: Geneva Press, 1999), especially chapter 3.

In Luke's Gospel the embodied fulfillment of God's promises, Jesus, is a living call for those who follow him to fear not and to live a life of joyful freedom released from the anxieties produced by fear (see Wheeler, 68–72). In the face of a world that sells fear and anxiety, Jesus offers joy, freedom, and a worry-free life based on trust in God. Possessions do not free but bind us to their care, while being bound to God frees us to lives full of joy and grace.

Questions for Reflection

1. The man in this story gained his wealth through legitimate means, not through theft or criminal activity. What is wrong with his desire to "relax, eat, drink, be merry"?
2. Is your church reluctant to talk about money? Why do you think this is? What can be done to make the topic less taboo?
3. In this passage Jesus tells his disciples, "Do not worry about your life, what you will eat, or about your body, what you will wear." Is that a difficult statement for you to practice?
4. As Dietrich Bonhoeffer said, "earthly possessions dazzle our eyes and delude us into thinking that they can provide security and freedom from anxiety. Yet all the time they are the very source of all anxiety." Has this ever been true in your life? If so, how?

Table Manners

One of the most intriguing scenes of the blockbuster movie *Titanic* revolves around a dinner in the first-class cabin. Jack, the main protagonist of the story and a third-class passenger on the giant ship, has been invited to dine at the table of Rose, whom he had kept from committing suicide the previous evening. Upon entering the elegant dining room, Jack enters a sparkling new world of manners, customs, and etiquette. Jack's dinner companions are all from the first-class cabins of the *Titanic* and are a little bemused by their guest; they don't know quite what to make of him. Most tolerate him, while some act as if they are waiting for him to show his "true colors" as the moment arrives when Jack is unaware of the customs for their dinner table. Looking at the table he finds utensils splaying out in all directions and wonders where to start, until a fellow diner suggests that he begin on the outside and work his way to the middle.

In the movie, Jack's smooth handling of the table situation is used to highlight his suave and debonair manner, which increases the favorable impression that is being built around him for the audience. His situation, however, is one that many people have encountered as they have gathered at table where they are not quite familiar with the customs of the land. It seems that at the table we encounter the essence of a society's understanding about social relations and proper manners. For most children it is at meals where social conditioning and the learning of appropriate and inappropriate behavior occurs: "Don't talk with your mouth full." "Did I say that you could be excused?" "What's the magic word? That's right, *please* pass the salt and pepper." "Did I say you could eat yet? We have not said grace for this meal." Most people probably remember the importance of being

65

a member of the "clean plate club," or of not slurping their soup, as part of their childhood.

Meals are occasions where the family gathers and learns what it means to be family. It is at the table that we learn the importance of saying thanks for the food we are given. It is at the table that we learn to treat others with respect by saying please and thank you. It is at the table where some of the most important information about being a part of something larger than ourselves, a family or community, is shared.

Luke 14 allows us to look in at Jesus' table manners and listen to his table talk. The setting of chapter 14 is a Sabbath meal at the house of a Pharisee, and Jesus has been invited to join the gathering. Throughout the Gospel, Luke informs us that Jesus breaks bread with all sorts of people (see Luke 5:29; 7:36; 11:37; 22:14; 24:30), so that one of the chief accusations brought against Jesus is that he, a proper religious person, has the audacity to eat and drink with sinners and tax collectors (Luke 5:30ff.). Just as the meal with the outcasts of his society highlights Jesus' message of hope, Jesus' table manners and table talk become emblematic, throughout Luke's Gospel, of the key tenets within his kingdom message. "Table talk was not only a fairly common literary device for gathering and disseminating discussions on a range of topics, but banquets did, in fact, provide occasions for philosophers and teachers to impart their wisdom" (Craddock, 175). In the Gospel of Luke, Jesus' being at table, the people with whom he eats, and what he says and does are all clues to understanding the person and work of Jesus. So it is no surprise that in Luke 14 we find Jesus at the house of a Pharisee preparing to engage in the Sabbath meal.

> "Table talk was not only a fairly common literary device for gathering and disseminating discussions on a range of topics, but banquets did, in fact, provide occasions for philosophers and teachers to impart their wisdom. However, for Judaism, for Jesus, and for the early church, table fellowship was laden with very important meanings, religious, social, and economic."—Fred B. Craddock, *Luke*, Interpretation, 175.

The Sabbath and Mercy (14:1–6)

In Luke 14:1–24, there are four scenes that follow the announcement that Jesus had been invited to dine with a leader of the Pharisees. Each of these scenes assumes a "table" setting, a place of learning about important social customs and central elements of Jesus' message. As the story is told, there is a hint that the contentious nature of the relationship between Jesus and the Pharisees (see Luke 5:21; 7:30; 11:37–54) continues even in the invitation for a meal. The text informs us that the Pharisees were watching Jesus very closely—a term which, elsewhere in Luke's Gospel, has indicated that they were looking for a way to accuse Jesus (Luke 6:7). So we do not know whether Jesus' encounter with the man with dropsy, a condition that today would probably be called edema and is related to excess fluid in the body, is a coincidence or a trap set by Jesus' opponents.

In either case, Jesus engages his audience by asking a question: "Is it lawful to cure people on the sabbath, or not?" (Luke 14:3). Already within Luke's Gospel, Jesus has confronted the Pharisees with regard to healing on the Sabbath (6:6–11 and 13:10–17), and in each case Jesus has acted to heal on the Sabbath. Jesus appears to be operating under a Sabbath understanding that comes from the tradition delineated in Deuteronomy 5:12ff. Within the two versions of the Ten Commandments (Exodus 20 and Deuteronomy 5), the only commandment that changes significantly from one version to the next is the Sabbath commandment. According to the Exodus text, the Sabbath is to be remembered because it is part of the natural order, and lack of Sabbath keeping threatens God's creation intentions (Ex. 20:8–11). In the version from Deuteronomy, however, the Sabbath is to be observed because it marks the redemptive release of Israel from the bondage of slavery to Pharaoh (Deut. 5:12–15). Thus, actions that are redemptive on the Sabbath, like healing a person afflicted with an illness, would be in keeping with the Sabbath trajectory arising out of this tradition (see also Isa. 56:1–8; Luke 13:16).

In response to Jesus' actions the Pharisees are dumbfounded and silent, perhaps suggesting that Jesus has "won the day" with regard to these Sabbath controversies (Ringe, 194). In the broader context, however, the healing on the Sabbath sets the stage for the table talk that will follow. Jesus embodies the redemptive power of God, a power that will overturn and upset the societal norms and expectations. Just as his healing on the Sabbath restores the man with dropsy to the community, the talk around the table will also center on inclusion in the kingdom community of God.

Guest Etiquette (14:7–11)

As the guests who have been invited to the Pharisee's house gather around the table, Jesus notices their actions and begins to teach. Jesus sees that they all have chosen the places of honor, so he tells them a parable. As often is the case, the simple and ordinary provides a "teachable moment" for Jesus to share the news of the kingdom. One wonders how many "teachable moments" we miss with those around us, especially children, because we are unaware and not looking for God to be present in the ordinary.

By using the term *parable,* Luke pushes us to see the story that Jesus tells as more than simply good advice on how not to be embarrassed at dinner parties. The custom in Jesus' time was for the guests to seat themselves around the table according to their respective honor in relation to the host; the guest with the most honor would sit nearest the host and the guest with the least would be farthest away. Reflecting this practice, Jesus' parable suggests that upon arriving at a banquet one should not sit in a place of honor, but be humble and sit at the far end of the table. Then if the host asks you to move up, you will receive honor, whereas if the host asks you to move down, you will suffer shame.

"Jesus does not offer a divinely approved way for a person to get what he or she wants. Taking the low seat because one is humble is one thing; taking the low seat as a way to move up is another. This entire message becomes a cartoon if there is a mad, competitive rush for the lowest place, with ears cocked toward the host, waiting for the call to ascend."—Fred B. Craddock, *Luke,* Interpretation, 177.

Since this is a parable, we are reminded that more is going on here than social advice: "This entire message becomes a cartoon if there is a mad, competitive rush for the lowest place, with ears cocked towards the host, waiting for a call to ascend" (Craddock, 177). Jesus concludes this scene with a saying about humility, which becomes a possible interpretive lens for the entire teaching: "For all who exalt themselves will be humbled, and those who humble themselves will be exalted" (Luke 14:11). At God's wedding banquet, kingdom principles rule and those who exalt themselves will be humbled, while those who enter in humility will be raised. Pride, privilege, and receiving one's perceived acclaim are not elements of God's kingdom. Jesus will conclude another parable in Luke 18:10–14 with this same statement about humility, as he compares the piety of a Pharisee, who seems to know his exalted status, and the tax collector, who realizes his utter unworthiness before God. Here at the Pharisee's banquet, Jesus reminds the guests that humility, especially at the banquet God will host, is characteristic of kingdom people.

Host Etiquette (14:12–14)

Turning from the guests to the host, Jesus continues his table talk. The guests have been corrected in their view of appropriate etiquette for the kingdom; they have been told that pride, position, and power are not important calling cards at God's banquet. Instead, humility and awe in the face of the host are important. As he shifts his gaze to his Pharisee host, Jesus continues the reversals that characterize his teaching for guests. Even today, most dinner party guests are of the same social status and class as the host. There is even the odd thought that if the Joneses are invited to the Smiths' party, then the Smiths are obligated to invite the Joneses to their party. So although hosting a banquet may be seen as wonderful act of hospitality, power plays and debt collection can also go into party planning, as the guest list may involve obligations to be paid and the desire to put others in one's debt (Craddock, 177).

Jesus begins this section of teaching by listing the usual guests at luncheons and dinners: friends, brothers and sisters, other relatives, rich neighbors. Each of these people can repay the hosts by inviting them to their own party at another time. These are guests, however, who are not to be requested to come to the party. Instead, Jesus suggests that one should invite "the poor, the crippled, the lame, and the blind" to the banquet, because they are not in a position to pay back the host. We have already seen that this list of guests is significant in Jesus' life, as he has based his ministry around them (e.g., Luke 4:18–19; 7:22ff.). These guests offer no promise of return, no future dinner party for the host to attend, but inviting them is much like God's invitation to the heavenly banquet. Fred Craddock writes, "[I]n the kingdom God is the host, and who can repay God? Jesus is therefore calling for kingdom behavior, that is, inviting to table those with neither property nor place in society. Since God is host of us all, we as hosts are really behaving as guests, making no claims, setting no conditions, expecting no return" (Craddock, 177).

To his hosts and their guests Jesus has offered a new reality shaped by the kingdom of God. The new reality is marked by humility and hospitality, essential characteristics for those who will gather at the heavenly banquet. Those who lack humility (Luke 18:10ff.) and hospitality (Luke 16:19ff.) will be judged wanting, but those who practice these disciplines will be invited guests at the great banquet prepared by God.

The Great Banquet (14:15–24)

Upon hearing Jesus' words on hospitality and humility, one of the guests at the Pharisee's banquet chimes in: "Blessed is anyone who will eat bread in the kingdom of God!" Given the nature of the earlier comments and the audience around Jesus, most understand that this guest includes himself as one of those who will sit at God's banquet table. Yet the nature of the parable that follows shows that Jesus responds to this self-assurance in such a way as to put on notice all who consider themselves shoo-ins for the kingdom.

Over the centuries, the most common way to understand this parable has been to allegorize it, that is, to assign a real-life person or group to each particular imaginary character within the story. So, the host of the banquet represents God; the guests who turn down the invitation are the Jews who refuse Jesus; and the outcasts who finally come to the banquet are the Gentiles. While the parable may have functioned within the early church along these lines as they began to take the good news of the gospel to Gentiles, an exact one-to-one allegorization raises problems, as each detail in the text must then be accounted for in the allegory. For instance, what is the difference between the first round of outcast invitees and the second? Are some Gentiles close and others farther away? What do we do with the host's anger and the presence of a slave? In light of these difficulties and the way that we have suggested parables work by inviting us into imaginary worlds, we will look at the primary characters in the story in their narrative setting, not moving outside of the parable until the end.

> "The invitation is continually being extended. The Lord of the banquet is continually sending out messengers. They come in the form of other people, of circumstances, and of our own inward insights countless times each day."—Alyce M. McKenzie, *Matthew*, Interpretation Bible Studies (Louisville, Ky.: Geneva Press, 1998), 80.

The first character we meet is the host. For whatever reason, this host is throwing a great banquet. According to custom, the host has sent invitations earlier to the guests, and now that the banquet is prepared, the final summons to the guests has gone out. For whatever reasons, these guests cannot come to the banquet (see below), and the host receives this news as a slap in the face. In view of this rejection, the host, although angry, widens the guest list and pulls in the most improbable people for the banquet—the poor, the crippled, the lame, the blind, and those on the highways and byways. The host has prepared the banquet, and when the original guests reject the final invitation to come and feast, others will be brought to the table graciously and freely.

The next group of major characters we meet are the three guests who reject the final call to come to the banquet. As noted earlier, ancient custom included sending out an invitation early in order to get the date on the guest's calendar, and then sending a summons when the banquet was ready. These three invitees know about the upcoming banquet, but the cares of the world get in the way of

Whom do we invite to our feasts?

their attendance, cares ranging from new property to a new wife. It is important to note that these excuses are legitimate, not last-minute escapes to avoid the party. "We are not here listening to worn-out stories about faulty alarm clocks, heavy traffic, noisy neighbors hindering sleep, misplaced calendars, or tardy car pools" (Craddock, 179). These valid excuses keep the three original invitees from attending the banquet and enjoying the feast.

The final group of characters that are presented are the new invitees. These invitees are portrayed as the outcasts in society, those who usually have no social standing and normally would not make the guest list of most banquets—the poor, lame, crippled, and blind. With these words, the eyebrows of those who have read Luke's Gospel lift up in recognition; these are the ones for whom Jesus has come and to whom he is bringing the good news of the kingdom. As Mary proclaimed earlier in her song, the hungry are being filled with good things (Luke 1:53). These guests receive the invitation out of the sheer grace of the host, who compels them to come in off the streets to

"Presumptions of privilege, whether on the basis of one's religious identity (seen in traditionally proper sabbath observance) or one's social status (seen in schemes to assure privilege or to protect one's economic status by business as usual), crumble in the face of the invitation to drop everything that contributes to one's system of security, and to join the party. For those who come, it is a splendid feast indeed."—Sharon H. Ringe, *Luke*, 200.

participate in the banquet. These are probably not the types of guests that the original inquirer expected would be at the kingdom banquet.

Jesus closes this section by boldly proclaiming that none of the invited guests will be joining his banquet, that is, the banquet of God. With this closing and the material that surrounds Jesus' description of the banquet, at least two topics are raised. The first topic is the danger of pride and of assuming that being an invited guest assures one of a place at the banquet. "The forces against which God's offer contends are reasonable and well argued, but God's offer has priority not simply over our worst but also over our best agendas" (Craddock, 179). Jesus' table talk speaks words of warning to the proud and self-assured: Do not assume too much and keep your priority on the banquet, not other matters. The second topic is the amazing nature of the kingdom of God, which offers and compels the undeserving to come and sit at the table and feast joyfully with God.

Want to Know More?

About biblical depictions of banquets and feasts? See Paul J. Achtemeier, ed., *HarperCollins Bible Dictionary*, rev. ed. (San Francisco: HarperSanFrancisco, 1996), 101–2, 333–35.

About healing on the Sabbath? See Michael R. Cosby, *Portraits of Jesus* (Louisville, Ky.: Westminster John Knox Press, 1999), 93.

In Christian tradition, the celebration of Communion is the foretaste of the coming feast in the kingdom. Luke 13:29 claims that people will come from east and west, north and south to sit at table in the kingdom of God. Different traditions practice Communion in different ways, but all agree that Christ is the real host, as it is the Lord's table. Luke 14 provides the table talk of the host who sets the manners for the banquet—help others, be humble, be hospitable. Christ is the host and we are the invited guests to the feast of feasts.

? Questions for Reflection

1. If "all who humble themselves will be exalted," how are we to avoid the "mad rush" for the lowest place at the table? What is the real message of Luke 14:7–11?
2. Parties and meals continue today to be places where "power plays and debt collection" are sometimes practiced. Have you ever gone over a guest list for a party you were throwing, marking off some names and adding others? What criteria did you use for adding or subtracting names?

3. Throughout his ministry Jesus found many "teachable moments" where he could share the gospel in meaningful ways. Are you aware of the different "teachable moments" in your life? Do you always take advantage of them?

4. Compare the three guests in Luke 14:18–20 to the "rich fool" in Luke 12:16–20, the priest and the Levite in Luke 10:30–37, and the would-be followers in Luke 9:59–62. What is similar about these characters? What is different? What does Jesus want us to learn about the kingdom of God from their actions?

8

Luke 15:1–32

Parables of the Lost

For many families, one of the favorite times of the evening is right after dinner. It is a time to catch up on the day, find out what is going on in the lives of other family members, and discuss important current issues. One pastor tells the story about what happened in one of those post-dinner conversations at his home. As they sat around the table, he asked, "Who is God?" After pausing to think and ponder, his three-year-old son Chris said, "You." Then, before he could revel in his new-found authority, Chris corrected his initial exclamation: "No. God is bigger than Godzilla." After they had finished laughing, the questioning continued: "Well, what is God like?" This time the oldest son chimed in, "God is nice, nice."

God is nice, nice. Adults have so many words that we use when we describe God: compassionate, just, immanent, transcendent, immortal, omnipresent, omnipotent, omniscient. These words are time-tested, theologically weighted, and bursting with implicit and explicit understanding. Yet these new words from a child catch us up with their simple poignancy: God is nice, nice.

As adults, we may wonder: is *nice* a word that we would use for God? What kind of God is *nice*? Does *nice* suggest a candy-coated God who does not have to be taken seriously? Does *nice* reduce the awesome majesty of God, trivializing God as something pleasant, palatable, and digestable? Does *nice* take the edge off of God? Looking in the dictionaries, one can find all sorts of meanings for nice: pleasant, as in the phrase "have a nice day"; done with subtlety and skill, as in "nice job"; of good character, respectable, as in "she is a nice person." Each of those may describe God: God is pleasant and acts with skill, and not many would challenge the character of God. Yet what is interesting is the origin of the word *nice*. It comes from the Latin word *nescius,* which means ignorant, foolish. Does saying that God is "nice, nice" mean God is foolish?

The pastor whose son had uttered the phrase "nice, nice" tried to determine what his son had meant; that is, he went back to the source in order to understand. So he turned back to his son and said: "What does it mean that God is nice, nice?" The son answered quickly and without pausing to think: "God is not mean. God forgives." A God who is nice, nice is a God who forgives. Is a God who forgives nice? Is a God who forgives foolish? Luke 15 explores the foolish grace of God that leads us to say that God is "nice, nice."

The Introduction (15:1–2)

Before moving into the parables that Jesus will tell, Luke provides his audience with a setting for the stories that follow. Tax collectors and sinners have joined the crowds that surround Jesus, which incites the Pharisees to "righteous" grumbling. With these lowly tax collectors and sinners in the crowd, the Pharisees sneer and say, "Look at him. Hmmph. He eats with 'those' people, those tax collectors. Those sinners."

Throughout Luke's Gospel, Jesus has been accused of hanging around the wrong kinds of people—tax collectors, sinners, and other socially dislocated people (Luke 5:30; 7:22–23; 19:1ff.). The danger of these associations was the danger of guilt by association, captured in the old saying, "Birds of a feather flock together." By association, the authority of Jesus is being called into question by the "righteous" people of his day. Jesus, the Messiah and the Son of God, should not be hanging around sinners, but should be with the "good" and "righteous" people. Luke reports earlier, however, that Jesus retorted to the critics of the company he kept: "Those who are well have no need of a physician, but those who are sick; I have come to call not the righteous but sinners to repentance" (Luke 5:31–32).

In Luke 15, Jesus once again confronts the claim that the "good and righteous" people make: "You're associating with the wrong kind of people." Intriguingly, one wonders

> "The Pharisees are not alone in believing that the separation of good and bad people preserves a community's sense of righteousness and is essential for the moral instruction of the young. Jesus' failure to observe such distinctions seemed to some dangerous to the moral and religious fiber of the community and disturbingly radical. It still is so regarded by some, even within the church."—Fred B. Craddock, *Luke,* Interpretation, 185.

if this accusation could still be made concerning the body of Christ today.

Jesus did not run away and hide from the "sinners," but welcomed them into his company and even sat at table with them (see unit 7 and the discussion of Luke 14:1–24). The story is told about a small city in the Midwest where a new X-rated video store was opened in the center of town. All the church people were outraged and met to remove this sinful presence from their midst, vilifying the owner as their anger increased. The pastor of one of the local churches, however, went into the store, met the owner, and befriended him, much to the chagrin of his parishioners. Eventually the store was closed, but the question raised by the action of the pastor echoes Jesus' question of the lawyer in Luke 10:36, "Which of these do you think was a neighbor to the man?"

Finding and Joy (15:3–10)

Hearing the accusations of the Pharisees, Jesus responds as he does throughout Luke's Gospel by telling parables, three, to be exact. The first two parables follow the same plot line, so we will look at them together. As with his other parables, Jesus pulls from the ordinary and everyday for discernment and enlightenment with regard to the kingdom of God. The crowds around Jesus would have been familiar with the context of these stories, and the stories would have rung true to their ears. Yet each parable also raises new imaginative possibilities for understanding God and God's kingdom.

In the first parable, one sheep out of a hundred has become separated from the other ninety-nine (see also Matt. 18:10–14). If the shepherd returns home with ninety-nine sheep, he finds himself still with 99 percent of his original flock, a percentage that most would find acceptable, and not worth the risk of looking for the one lost sheep. Yet the shepherd leaves the ninety-nine unguarded in the wilderness and finds the one lost sheep—an action that many would consider quite foolish. Similarly, the second parable tells of a woman who loses a coin and diligently searches until she finds it.

While the parables begin with loss, they end with being found, and the joyful celebrations that accompany the finding. Both the shepherd and the woman call together friends and neighbors and throw parties for that which was lost and now is found. The focus of the parables is on the joyous and exuberant party that is thrown, as Jesus ends both with a declaration about the heavenly celebration for the repentance and coming home of one sinner. When something or someone is lost and then found, great rejoicing occurs, and this rejoicing is reflective of the heavenly joy when one of God's children comes home. "Finding and restoring the lost gives pleasure to God as well as to all who are about God's business" (Craddock, 186).

> "Amazing grace, how sweet the sound, that saved a wretch like me. I once was lost but now am found, was blind but now I see."—John Newton, "Amazing Grace."

"A man who had two sons" (15:11–32)

This third parable has often been called the parable of the prodigal son, but as theologian and pastor Helmut Thielicke has pointed out, it is more a parable about the waiting father, which we capture in the first verse, "There was a man who had two sons" (Thielicke, 29). The parable tells its story with an economy of language and moves quickly through the action of the father and his two sons. Two parallel scenes involve the father and each of his sons respectively, beginning with the younger son and ending with the elder son. In both cases, the father's action remains the same. The sons, however, behave differently in their respective moments on the stage. Imagining the action of the parable on a stage is an effective way to read this particular passage, as the people who speak and would be on stage form the center of the respective scenes.

The first scene begins with the younger son rejecting the security and love of his father's house by demanding that his inheritance be given to him. Many have noted that this demand is tantamount to wishing that his father were dead, but the father gives him the inheritance. The son, flush with newfound wealth, goes to a far country, spends his money quickly, and finds himself destitute and literally living with pigs. For Jesus' Jewish audience, being forced to eat and live with pigs would be about as low as one could get, given the unclean nature of these animals. The younger son finds himself at a low point, eating the carob pods that provide the fodder for the pigpen. In the midst of the muck, he decides to return home, beg for mercy, and become a hired hand in his father's household. He does not expect a restoration, but would like to be received at the lowest station in his father's household, for even that would be better than his life with the pigs.

All of this happens quickly in the first few lines of the parable, but then the action slows down as the primary character comes into focus. It is the father, who apparently has been waiting for the return of the son. At the son's approach to the homestead, the waiting father rushes

out to meet him. As they come together, the younger son tries to blurt out his rehearsed speech of repentance, hopefully seeking mercy, but the father is quicker. In rapid, staccato succession the father embraces his son and calls first for a robe, then a ring, and finally shoes, which are visible signs that this one is a treasured child, not a hired hand. The father continues the celebration of his lost son's homecoming with a giant banquet. Like the parties for the found sheep and found coin, here is a party of great joy for the child who was lost and now is found. Instead of exacting penance or giving some long "sermon" about wasted wealth and time, the father extravagantly welcomes home the one who has been gone.

After noting the extravagant "coming home" party for the younger son, Jesus continues the parable and the listeners find themselves confronted with a second father-son encounter and the response of the elder son. The elder son has been working in the field, and as he is "coming home" he hears the party and sends a servant to find out what in the world is going on back at home. Rather quickly the servant reports to the elder brother that his younger brother has returned. Moreover, and this is the surprising part, his father has killed the fatted calf and a joyful, extravagant party is being thrown. In response to all that the servant tells him, the elder son becomes angry and refuses to join the celebration.

Too many times the elder has been painted as a spoilsport or as "a hard-hearted miser who never learned to dance" (Craddock, 188). But there is more going on here. The elder son is not a caricature; nor is he easily dismissed. Many have noted that he is just as lost as his younger brother, but he has become lost without leaving home. This can be seen in the elder brother's response to the father who comes out to meet him. The elder complains that he has always been faithful, that he has always been diligent, that he has never been a slacker, and has never gone astray from his father's guidance. Despite all his hard work and the way he has stayed home and done "what is right," the father has offered neither party nor extravaganza. The way the elder brother describes his faithfulness, however, turns what should have been a joyful sharing of life in the father's house into years of drudgery and uninspired obedience. Moreover, the elder brother is affronted by the foolish extravagance of his father's grace toward the wayward brother. It may have been okay to welcome his younger brother back, but his father did not have to throw a party for him. Perhaps after a few days living in the shed out back, a few days of not sharing in the family meals, and a few other acts of penance and contrition, the younger brother could return to the family's graces. Throwing an extravagant and exuberant party should not be in the cards for the "lost" one, according to the elder brother. It might be said that the father is rather foolish.

Before moving on, it is important to recall the setting that Luke has provided for Jesus in telling these parables. The good religious folk including the Pharisees are uncomfortable and downright upset about the company of people that surround Jesus, especially the tax collectors and sinners. While we often perceive ourselves as the prodigal who has returned home, the story of the elder brother causes good, religious folk to do a double take. In his book *The Return of the Prodigal Son,* Henri Nouwen, an author known for his work on spirituality, notes that we often find ourselves in the position of the elder brother:

> "The bite of the [parable of the prodigal son] is felt primarily by people of privilege, especially those who see themselves as relentlessly good and faithful, and so as deserving the blessings they enjoy. In fact, we probably side with the younger brother only because we know the outcome of the parable ahead of time. In our heart of hearts we know that the older brother has a point, and we grumble too at love that makes a home for both sons."—Sharon H. Ringe, *Luke,* Westminster Bible Companion, 209–10.

All of this became very real for me when a friend who had recently become a Christian criticized me for not being very prayerful. His criticism made me very angry. I said to myself, "How dare he teach me a lesson about prayer! For years he lived a carefree and undisciplined life, while I since childhood have scrupulously lived the life of faith. Now he is converted and starts telling me how to behave!" This inner resentment reveals to me my own lostness. I had stayed home and did not wander off, but had not yet lived a free life in my father's house. (Nouwen, 70)

As Nouwen suggests, the elder son felt anger, resentment, and a lack of joyous response because he was shocked by the foolish grace of his father. His father was being too *nice* to the rascal who had blown all his money.

In her short story "Revelation," Flannery O'Connor introduces her readers to Mrs. Turpin, a middle-class white lady in the deep South of the mid-twentieth century, and perhaps another image of the elder brother. For Mrs. Turpin, everyone has a place, and her own place is in the upper echelon. She looks with some disgust at people she believes are beneath her, including those she calls "white trash" and the blacks in her town. Mrs. Turpin's husband, Claud, had been injured by a cow on their farm and they find themselves in a doctor's waiting room. As they wait, Mrs. Turpin, both internally and externally with snide comments, sizes up everyone in the room, finding all of them inadequate. This is not by any fault of their own, however, Mrs. Turpin believes. Looking around the room, she finds some solace in the thought that her lot is not that of anyone else in the room.

> "If it's one thing I am," Mrs. Turpin said with feeling, "it's grateful. When I think who all I could have been besides myself and what all I got, a little of everything and a good disposition besides, I just feel like shouting, 'Thank you Jesus for making everything the way it is!' It could have been different!" (O'Connor, 499)

In response to this soliloquy, a young college girl who had gone away to school up north, another failing that Mrs. Turpin notes, throws a book at Mrs. Turpin. The mother of the young woman and the nurse end up having to restrain the girl, and she is eventually sedated, but before the sedative works she shouts, "Go back to hell where you came from, you old wart hog."

As the doctor tends to the gash in Mrs. Turpin's head, the other people in the room provide the judgment on the act of the college girl, who, they agree, must be a "lunatic." As she goes home, however, Mrs. Turpin finds that she cannot so easily dismiss the words of the "crazy" college girl. The words haunt her and briefly force her to examine the structure of reality that she has built. She thinks of how she treats the black men who work on her

"And bringing up the end of the procession [were those] who had always had a little of everything and the God-given wit to use it right. . . . They were marching behind the others with great dignity, accountable as they had always been for good order and common sense and respectable behavior. They alone were on key. Yet she could see by their shocked and altered faces that even their virtues were being burned away."—Flannery O'Connor, "Revelation," in *The Complete Stories* (New York: Farrar, Straus & Giroux, 1972), 508.

farm, and how she judges others as inferior to her. This only lasts for a moment, however, as she reminds herself that the girl was a "lunatic" and really *did* belong in an asylum. Even though she "comes to her senses," the words from the waiting room continue to haunt Mrs. Turpin, until finally she has a vision standing by the pigpen of her farm:

> A visionary light settled in her eyes. . . . Upon it a vast horde of souls were rumbling toward heaven. There were whole companies of white-trash, clean for the first time, and bands of black[s] in white robes, and battalions of freaks and lunatics shouting and clapping and leaping like frogs. And bringing up the end of the procession was a tribe of people whom she recognized at once as those who, like herself and Claud, had always had a little of everything and the God-given wit to use it right. She leaned forward to observe them closer. They were marching behind the others with great dignity, accountable as they had always been for good order and common sense and respectable behavior. They alone were on key. Yet she could see by their shocked and altered faces that even their virtues were being burned away. (O'Connor, 508)

Like Mrs. Turpin, the elder son in the parable of the waiting father is not left without an alternative vision. As he did with the younger son, so the father does with the elder. We have already noted that he goes out to greet him, as he had gone out to greet the younger son. He goes out to bring him into the circle, to invite him to join the party, to welcome him home as his son. In his response to the elder son, the father tries to help him see the world through a different interpretive lens. Whereas the elder saw life with the father as unrewarded drudgery, the father posits that the son has been with him daily and what a joy that is. Whereas the elder resents the extravagance of the party, the father reminds the elder that everything of the father's has been and will be the elder's. The father ends his discussion with the elder brother with words that echo the earlier rejoicing over the found sheep and found coin. Like the shepherd and the woman, the father says, "But we had to celebrate and rejoice, because this brother of yours was dead and has come to life; he was lost and has been found" (Luke 15:32).

Want to Know More?

About the use of shepherds in parables? See Paul J. Achtemeier, ed., *HarperCollins Bible Dictionary*, rev. ed. (San Francisco: HarperSanFrancisco, 1996), 1012–13.

About the prodigal son? See Robert H. Stein, *An Introduction to the Parables of Jesus* (Philadelphia: Westminster Press, 1981), 115–24.

The first scene sets the pattern for what will follow. A son finds himself disconnected from the father's house for whatever reason. Upon returning to the father's house, the son is met by the father, who warmly receives him and invites the son into the house for a joyous celebration. The love for the younger son does not cancel out the father's love for the elder son. The father invites both of his lost sons back to the house, to come home for the feast. The parable ends, however, without revealing the elder son's response to the father's invitation. This ending is an invitation, however, for those who hear it, to finish the story in their minds. Is the father's grace too exuberant and too foolish, so that the elder remains outside, offended and upset by the forgiveness offered his younger brother? Or is grace too exuberant and too foolish, so that the elder joins in the celebration for the one who was lost and has been found?

Who is God? God is a God who foolishly welcomes us home, the prodigals who have gone astray, and throws a foolish party for our return. God is also one who invites us to the party, the elder sons and daughters, and opens our hearts again to the joy of the feasts of heaven. God forgives us, young and old alike, and bids us come home. It seems that God truly is nice, nice.

? Questions for Reflection

1. Is it still true of Christians today that we "associate with the wrong kind of people"? What do you think this means? Who are the tax collectors of our day?
2. Read again the two parables in Luke 15:3–10. What famous hymn do they bring to mind? What do they tell us about God's love for God's children?
3. Much like the parable of the good Samaritan discussed in unit 5, the full message of the parable of the prodigal son is often overlooked, as we are inclined to either ignore or demonize the older brother. Why do you think this is?
4. Have there been times in your life when you've felt like the prodigal son? Like the older son? Like the father?

Reflections from the Cross: The Death of Jesus

For since, in the wisdom of God, the world did not know God through wisdom, God decided, through the foolishness of our proclamation, to save those who believe. For Jews demand signs and Greeks desire wisdom, but we proclaim Christ crucified, a stumbling block to Jews and foolishness to Gentiles, but to those who are the called, both Jews and Greeks, Christ the power of God and the wisdom of God. For God's foolishness is wiser than human wisdom, and God's weakness is stronger than human strength.

—1 Corinthians 1:21–25

I believe . . . in Jesus Christ his only Son our Lord . . . who suffered under Pontius Pilate, was crucified, dead, and buried.

—The Apostles' Creed

For I handed on to you as of first importance what I in turn had received: that Christ died for our sins in accordance with the scriptures.

—1 Corinthians 15:3

The crucifixion of Jesus is the central event in the proclamation of the Gospels, Paul's letters, and the confessions of the churches throughout the centuries. In each of the canonical Gospels, the movement of the narrative flows through the Galilean ministry, through the parables and healings, and through the times of prayer and times of action, toward Jesus' eventual execution upon a Roman cross as a criminal. Luke, for instance, records at least three direct instances where Jesus predicts his coming betrayal and death (Luke 9:22, 44; 18:32–33). For Paul and the early church, this event was the primary focus of preaching and teaching.

Given the centrality of this event for Christian witness and proclamation, it is rather interesting to find the actual description of the immediate events around the crucifixion to be recorded briefly and sparsely. Compared to the rest of their Gospels, Matthew, Mark, Luke, and John spend little time on the crux moment in the story (see Matt. 27:32–56; Mark 15:21–41; Luke 23:26–49; and John 19:16–37). While the Gospels agree on the outline of the events—such as the mocking soldiers, the sign nailed on the cross, the place of execution, and Jesus' speaking from the cross—they differ somewhat in the words that Jesus speaks and the reactions of those around Jesus. These differences help highlight the emphases of each of these Gospels and provide four different interpretive lenses on the significance of Jesus' death. The last words of Jesus upon the cross provide a central clue regarding these different emphases. For Matthew and Mark, Jesus' last understandable cry is one of anguished alienation and a quote of Psalm 22, "My God, My God, why have you forsaken me?" (Matt. 27:46; Mark 15:34). For John, Jesus' last audible words are "It is finished," pointing to John's assertion that Jesus' ascending upon the cross is equivalent to his ascending upon the throne of God (John 19:30).

> "Of course, the followers of Jesus found it extremely difficult to pronounce the words, 'Jesus is dead'; the church always has. To this day, some churches withhold nothing in the celebration of Easter, while not marking at all Good Friday, as though there could be a resurrection without a corpse."—Fred B. Craddock, *Luke*, Interpretation, 278.

In his description of the events of Jesus' execution, Luke walks a middle ground between the anguish of Matthew and Mark and the utter assurance of John. Luke provides details that are unavailable in the other Gospels concerning the final conversation between Jesus and those crucified with him, as well as in the response of those who witness the event. Whereas Matthew and Mark record only one saying of Jesus from the cross, both John (John 19:26–7, 28, 30) and Luke (Luke 23:34, 43, 46) have three sayings that are unique to their respective Gospels. For Luke, the final three statements of Jesus on the cross, as well as the responses spoken and unspoken by the crucifixion witnesses, sum up the central tenets of the Gospel and set the stage for the church's future ministry as recorded in Luke's sequel, the book of Acts.

"Father, forgive them; for they do not know what they are doing" (23:32–38)

As has been the case earlier where he forms central instances of Jesus' life into groups of three, Luke provides three vignettes surrounding

"Father, forgive them . . ."

the final moments of Jesus' earthly existence (Luke 23:32–38, 39–43, 44–49). Each of these vignettes provides insight into Luke's proclamation to Theophilus about Jesus as the embodied fulfillment of God's saving activity.

In the first vignette, Luke informs the reader that Jesus has been led away with two other criminals to a place called "The Skull," where all three are crucified. Descriptions of the brutality and horror of crucifixion as a means of execution abound, as it makes for a slow and extremely painful death that eventually comes through suffocation. Setting the scene a little more, Luke briefly notes that the other criminals are crucified on the left and right of Jesus. As Jesus hangs on the cross, some cast lots for his garments while others mock him with disparaging remarks echoing the earlier words of Satan in Luke 4:1–13, "If you are the Son of God, then . . ." (see also Ps. 22:7–8, 18).

Taking a step back, it is important to note the scandal of this narrative. Jesus, the one we call Lord and Savior, is being treated like a common criminal—executed and mocked. Messiahs are not supposed to die as executed convicts; yet here is Jesus upon a cross. Paul called Jesus' crucifixion a "stumbling block" for some and noted that it would appear as "foolishness" to others. It ought to give us pause, if we so easily accept the crucifixion as just another piece of the story and do not deal with the horror and pain of this moment. The cross reminds us that Christianity at its best is not an escapist religion, but one that engages the best and worst of our lives.

In this first vignette, the mockings of Jesus by the leaders of the people and the soldiers form the key reactions of those witnessing Jesus' death. We have already seen that their words echo the earlier words of Satan, as in both cases Jesus is challenged to prove his divine sonship by saving himself. Yet the mocking words of the leaders and then the soldiers point to Luke's central claims concerning the identity of Jesus. They use the terms "Messiah of God," "chosen one," and "king of the Jews," so that unwittingly they witness to Jesus' true nature. While the leaders and the soldiers mock Jesus, the crowd who had vocally called for his crucifixion in Luke 23:18–23 is silent in the face of the cross.

In response to all that is going on around him, perhaps both the mocking and the silence, Jesus speaks and says: "Father, forgive them; for they do not know what they are doing" (Luke 23:34). As Luke tells the story of Jesus, he continually points to forgiveness as being a key to understanding Jesus and the path he calls his followers to tread. The Pharisees and others accuse Jesus of blasphemy because he forgives sins (Luke 5:20ff.). The disciples wonder at Jesus when he forgives the sins of a prostitute who has anointed his feet (Luke 7:48–50). When asked for a model prayer, Jesus places forgiveness right in the middle of what will become known as the Lord's Prayer (Luke 11:2–4). Later, Jesus suggests that we should forgive, not seven times but seven times seventy, brothers and sisters who sin against us and repent (Luke 17:4). Luke is the only Gospel that reports that on the cross Jesus said: "Father, forgive them; for they do not know what they are doing." In the midst of the violence of the cross, without a proper repentance, on that Good Friday so long ago, Jesus boldly declares that God forgives: "Father, forgive them."

Yet our experience tells us that forgiveness is difficult. It is so difficult that the text in many modern translations is footnoted, and the footnote tells us that many ancient manuscripts of Luke's Gospel omit the phrase, "Father forgive them, for they do not know what they are doing." Before the days of the printing press and the book, each text had to be hand-copied, and many of those ancient copies did not include Jesus' words of forgiveness from the cross. Why? Why would this central statement of Jesus be absent from the text? While various reasons have been proposed, many believe it was excised because it was a statement difficult enough to believe, but impossible to practice with hated enemies (Brown, 973–81). Perhaps in their reflections some early Christians said, "How could Jesus forgive those who killed him and how can we, his early church, forgive those same groups, the Romans and the Jews, who persecute and kill us?" So they excised the text, removed it, cut it away.

Forgiveness is so central to our faith, yet so difficult to practice. Difficult enough that some would remove it from Luke's text, yet it remains and thus continues to be central for lives of discipleship. In the ultimate moment of agony, Christ forgives. Forgiveness is central, but experience tells us it is difficult. It is our call, but how it is practiced is difficult. It cannot be trivialized or glossed over, but requires hard work and sacrifice.

In the late 1980s a movie called *The Mission* came out about Jesuit missionaries in South America, starring Robert DeNiro and Jeremy Irons. In the middle of the movie, one sequence of events poignantly depicts the centrality and difficulty of forgiveness. In the film, set in the colonial period, Irons portrays a Jesuit leader whose order has converted a group of indigenous people to the Christian faith and established among them an almost paradisaical community based on Christian principles. DeNiro plays a slaver, one who trapped, stole, dehumanized, and exported the same Indians to Portugal. Through a series of events, the swashbuckling DeNiro finds himself in jail for killing his brother in a jealous rage over a woman. As he sits in prison, all the sins of exploitation and murder haunt DeNiro until he is a completely broken man.

Irons, as a priest, comes and offers him a chance for new life. DeNiro refuses. There is no forgiveness that Irons can offer or that DeNiro can accept for the evil he has perpetrated. Yet Irons persists and finally DeNiro agrees to leave, but a powerful penance—a visible sign of repentance—is agreed to: DeNiro's shining armor, sword, shield, the trappings of his former life, are placed in a net and tied to DeNiro so that wherever he goes he must drag this weight of the past visibly with him. Irons and DeNiro leave the jail, the city, and return to the jungle and the Indian village. The way is arduous and perilous, over mountains and rivers. Yet through it all DeNiro drags the armor. The other priests of Irons's order complain that the penance is too hard and even try to remove the burden by cutting it away and throwing it down a hill. But DeNiro will not let it go. He runs down the hill and reattaches the net with the armor.

Finally, they reach the Indian village high in the mountainous jungle. Irons and the other Jesuits are the first to arrive; then the camera pans back to find DeNiro barely making it up the final path to encounter those whom he had tortured, whose daughters and fathers he had stolen. DeNiro collapses. He can go no farther. The weight of the past has won. Then one of the Indians takes a knife and goes down the hill, perhaps to kill the hated slaver. Drawing the knife over DeNiro, he cuts the cord, grabs the net, and tosses it into the river gorge. The Indian looks at DeNiro, helps him up, and brings him into the fellowship of the community.

Jesus' words of forgiveness reverberate through the centuries. They are a call for all who would follow in his steps to practice his words daily—"just as the Lord has forgiven you, so you also must forgive" (Col. 3:13). Forgiveness is so difficult, but it is so central to who we are.

"Today you will be with me in Paradise" (23:39–43)

Following the mocking of the soldiers and leaders, the second vignette narrows the focus of the spotlight on the three condemned men hanging on crosses. Of all the Gospels, Luke alone records a conversation between Jesus and the two criminals hanging beside him. The conversation moves from one criminal to another and finally concludes with a summary statement from Jesus.

The first voice to be heard is from one of the criminals, who joins his voice to the chorus of mocking from the previous scene: "Are you not the Messiah? Save yourself and us!" (Luke 23:39). Once again, unwittingly at that, the mocker has uttered key claims about Jesus as he challenges the reality that Jesus is a Messiah who can save. Throughout Luke's Gospel, Jesus has been portrayed as the one who saves, the Savior. In fact, Luke is the only one of the Synoptic Gospels to directly apply this term to Jesus, as the angels announcing his birth proclaim that a savior has been born in Bethlehem (Luke 2:11; see also 1:47; 7:50; 9:24; 19:10). Beginning with Mary's song (Luke 1:47–55) and moving throughout the rest of Luke, Jesus embodies God's plan of salvation, especially in turning the world upside down ("For all who exalt themselves will be humbled, and those who humble themselves will be exalted," Luke 14:11; also 18:14) and restoring those who for whatever reason have been lost ("For the Son of Man came to seek out and to save the lost," Luke 19:10; also see earlier discussions of Luke 10:25–37 in unit 5; 14:1–24 in unit 7; and 15:1–32 in unit 8). The assertions of the criminal on the cross join the cacophony of voices around the cross: "If you are a Savior, save! If you are what you say you are, save us and yourself!"

In response to these taunts, the other criminal speaks and rebukes the mocker. Picking up on themes that have played throughout Luke and will be highlighted again in the description of Jesus' actual death, the second criminal provides a witness to faith as he challenges the declarations of the first. The second criminal begins his faith statement by reminding the other criminal in so many words that the "fear of the LORD is the beginning of knowledge" (Prov. 1:7). This knowledge allows the second criminal to see that he and the mocker stand justly condemned for their actions, but Jesus has done nothing wrong. The narrative will pick up this assertion about the innocence of Jesus in the next section, but at this point in the narrative the second criminal has identified himself as a captive in need of release (recall Luke 4:18–19). He is condemned to die and in need of saving.

After dismissing the taunts of the first criminal, the second criminal addresses Jesus directly: "Remember me when you come into your kingdom" (Luke 23:42). In the beginning of Luke's Gospel, Mary's song of praise emphasizes the memory of God that will lead to the redemption of God's people. Here, the criminal seeks to align himself with that memory and to participate in the coming kingdom of salvation. Whereas the mockers witness to Jesus despite themselves, the penitent criminal provides a direct statement of belief that Jesus is the one who can save and that he indeed is the Messiah, the anointed one who will rule. In many ways, his is the cry of the faithful throughout the ages, and the inner yearning of all humans, that they will be remembered and not cut off from the presence of God (e.g., Pss. 13; 51:11). When facing the dark night of the soul and the crisis moments of our lives, we echo the criminal's plaintive plea: "Remember me . . ."

The promise and hope of the gospel seen clearly in Jesus, who is the primary physical evidence of the memory of God, is that God remembers and saves (see Gen. 8:1; 9:15; Ex. 2:24; 6:5). Jesus responds to the criminal, "Truly I tell you, today you will be with me in Paradise" (Luke 23:43). Often the study of Jesus' statement has been focused on trying to describe the nature of the paradise to which Jesus refers and the time frame of "life after death" captured in the word "today." While these questions are interesting, they move beyond the frame of the text. Throughout Luke's telling of the Gospel, "today" has been used to describe the immediacy and palpable presence of Jesus as the embodiment of salvation (Luke 2:11; 4:21; 19:9). Here the use suggests again that in, through, by, and because of the presence of Jesus, salvation occurs, and the criminal already participates in that salvation. In a similar manner, an exact location and description of "paradise" rests beyond the purview of this text, but the promise of the text is that because Jesus remembers, the criminal will be delivered, saved, and in the presence of God. Craddock comments, "Three times he [Jesus] has been mocked with 'Save yourself,' the one criminal adding 'and us.' Here Jesus does save someone, and that the one saved is a dying criminal is totally congenial to the types of persons blessed by Jesus throughout his ministry. In his own dying hour, Jesus continues his ministry" (Craddock, 274).

"Father, into your hands I commend my spirit" (23:44–49)

This final vignette records the actual death of Jesus. The cast of witnesses continues to include the soldiers and the crowds, but is expanded. The list of witnesses is first expanded to include nature itself. Luke informs his audience that Jesus was crucified at the noon hour, but instead of bright sunshine there is complete darkness. While many have tried to provide scientific explanations for this loss of light, Luke is primarily making a theological point. "The Scriptures frequently witness to the whole creation's involvement in those affairs which affect human history. . . . If stones cry out when disciples are silent (19:40), why would not the sky darken when the Son of God hangs dying?" (Craddock, 274).

> "In Luke's account, the moment of death leads not to a cry of God-forsakenness (Matt. 27:46; Mark 15:34), but to an equally strong cry declaring God's presence: 'Father, into your hands I commend my spirit' (23:46). With this prayerful quotation of Psalm 31:5, Luke portrays Jesus' faith in God as the God who saves, and having entrusted his spirit or breath (the Greek word means both) to God, Jesus dies."—Sharon H. Ringe, *Luke,* Westminster Bible Companion, 279.

Not only is the world crying out at the execution of Jesus, but Luke reports that the curtain in the Temple is rent in two. Unlike Matthew and Mark, who report this tearing of the curtain after Jesus actually dies, Luke reports the event prior to Jesus' last words. This has led to some confusion among interpreters over Luke's intent here, but many agree that Luke is pointing to the cross, saying: Here we see God clearly. The curtain served as a visual barrier to the "Holy of Holies" of the Temple in order to separate, which is a primary understanding of holiness in Hebrew thought, that area around the presence of God within the Temple. If the curtain were torn in two, God would be revealed. Given the convergence of the tearing of the curtain and Jesus hanging on the cross, Luke perhaps is making a statement that the Holy and awesome God is clearly seen in this man hanging on a cross. Throughout our study of Luke, we have seen that Jesus is the embodied presence of God's salvation—a salvation that operates in unexpected ways. Luke now confirms for his audience again in concurrence with these new nonhuman witnesses that Jesus is the Son of God.

As the story moves on, Luke narrows the focus of our attention directly on Jesus. In the Gospels of Matthew and Mark, Jesus' final understandable words are an anguished cry from Psalm 22, a psalm of lament. For Matthew and Mark, the suffering of the Messiah is a central tenet that challenges their audiences to reinterpret God and God's plan for humanity. For Luke, who throughout has kept the focus on God's plan incorporated in Jesus, the vision of the final moments of Jesus' life is different. Again and again, the audience of Luke's Gospel is informed that key moments were necessary for Jesus at certain times and places in his life (see Luke 2:49; 4:43; 13:16). Within that necessity, as if part of God's plan, is the fact that Jesus must suffer and die (e.g., Luke 9:22; 17:25; 22:37). The cross is part of the movement of God through history, a necessary part that is neither totally unexpected nor totally expected. With these final words, Luke reports the utter trust of Jesus in the presence of God even at death. Even here, at the cessation of life, God is present and available, which suggests that in a strange way God is there in all moments of utter helplessness and hopelessness. At times unseen and at other times clearly visible, God is there.

After his final word from the cross, Jesus dies. In response to his death, the people in the crowd, who earlier had clamored for his death and then stood in stunned silence during the gruesome execution, go home beating their breasts in a sign of intense mourning. Their movement from hostility to silence to mourning provides yet another witness to the power of Jesus' self-giving.

Not only are the crowds moved, but so is a soldier who has previously mocked and taunted Jesus. All the Synoptic Gospels report this final witness to Jesus' death and the change wrenched in the

> "When the centurion saw what had taken place, he praised God and said, 'Certainly this man was innocent.'"—Luke 23:47

centurion's perception. Watching how Jesus died, the centurion announces for the narrative: "Certainly this man was innocent."

91

With the play on one word (*just*), the statement of the centurion echoes the earlier statement of the criminal hanging beside Jesus. Whereas the criminal reminded his mocking friend that they had "justly" received their punishment, the centurion boldly proclaims that Jesus truly is "just" (NRSV: innocent). Once again, the cross and Jesus have changed the life of one who encountered them.

Luke reserves his final comment, however, for the acquaintances or friends of Jesus who, we are told for the first time, are witnesses to the crucifixion. As Luke tells the story, those closest to Jesus were those farthest away from him at his execution. Soldiers, the religious leaders, the crowds, and criminals surrounded Jesus, while his friends stood at a distance. From one angle, Luke may be suggesting the difficulty of being close to Jesus. Throughout the Gospel, Luke has highlighted the costs of discipleship and the crosses that the followers of Jesus must bear (see Luke 9:51–62). Perhaps through their distance Luke is reminding his audience of the pitfalls on the path laid for those who follow Jesus. To follow this one, you must weigh the cost. On the other hand, Luke may be setting the stage for those who will witness the resurrection by having them also witness the crucifixion (Craddock, 275). These friends will be the ones who bear witness not only to the crucified Christ but to the risen Lord.

Or perhaps Luke has his eyes on us. We too witness the final moments of Jesus' life from afar. We, like Theophilus, have gone along with Luke and have been brought to this moment that we might know the truth. We are the ones who hear and are now called to obey (Luke 8:21). We hear the final words of Jesus that say: God forgives, God saves, and God is present. The last witnesses to Jesus' death are those of us who stand at a distance from it, having encountered it through Luke's Gospel. Like Jesus' first acquaintances, we are called to hear and obey and to witness to the one "who was crucified, dead, and buried," but who also, on the third day, rose again.

Want to Know More?

About forgiveness? See *The Westminster Dictionary of Christian Theology* (Philadelphia: Westminster Press, 1983), 214–15.

About salvation? See *The Westminster Dictionary of Christian Theology*, 519–21.

About crucifixion in biblical times? See Paul J. Achtemeier, *HarperCollins Bible Dictionary*, rev. ed. (San Francisco: HarperSanFrancisco, 1996), 211–12.

? Questions for Reflection

1. Have someone in your group read aloud each of the Gospel accounts of the crucifixion—Matthew 27:32–56; Mark 15:21–41; Luke 23:32–49; John 19:16–37. Discuss the differences and similarities in the different accounts. Look specifically at Jesus' last recorded words from the cross (Matt. 27:46; Mark 15:34; Luke 23:46; John 19:30). Which of these Gospel accounts is easier for you to accept? Why?

2. Look back at unit 2 and the temptations of Jesus (Luke 4:1–30). Then reread Luke 23:35–39. How are the temptations in the wilderness similar to the temptations on the cross?

3. Who does Luke say watched the crucifixion "at a distance?" Why is this significant? What does it say about the cost of discipleship?

4. Some translators of the Bible note that Luke 23:34 was omitted in many ancient manuscripts, perhaps because Jesus' statement about forgiveness was so difficult to practice. How would our faith today be different if the statement had been completely lost over the centuries? Would it make our faith easier or more difficult? More meaningful, or less?

10 Luke 24:13–35

Along the Road to Emmaus

There is an old saying about an effective structure for a sermon or a speech of any type: tell them what you are going to say; say it to them; tell them what you said. While it may not be the most creative and exciting structure, it does focus the speaker on the central point of the presentation and drills that point into the hearer's consciousness. Although Luke was not familiar with this modern framework, his Gospel basically moves through these stages. In the birth and childhood narratives (Luke 1–3), Luke tells his audience what he is going to say: this child is going to be the promised redeemer (Luke 1:49–56) and Savior (Luke 2:11). Through angelic announcements to barren women and lowly shepherds, Luke informs his audience that what he is going to tell will be good news to those who are without power and status in society—the world will be turned upside down by this child.

Following the announcement of what he is going to say, Luke tells his audience who this Jesus is through a series of three movements: an itinerant ministry in Galilee (Luke 4:1–9:50), a journey to Jerusalem (Luke 9:51–19:28), and final events in and around Jerusalem (Luke 19:29–23:56). As we have seen earlier, throughout the first movement people inquire about who Jesus is, while the second movement lays out the parameters for those who would follow Jesus. In the final movement, the consummation of Jesus' identity and call to discipleship occur as he is tried, convicted, and crucified. In these three movements, Luke tells us the heart of his message: this crucified one is the Savior who redeems the world and calls his followers to obedient discipleship that will change their lives dramatically.

In chapter 24 we encounter Luke's retelling of what has been told.

Luke's final words, however, are not simply a final reiteration of the earlier news. The story that Luke has told to this point comes to an end as do many tales, with the death of the primary actor. The final news is the death of Jesus (Luke 23:46) and the dispersal of those who witnessed his execution (Luke 23:49–56). Even though Jesus had predicted his death, the finality, the reality, of death casts its pall over the final scenes in chapter 23. Chapter 24 will retell the story of this crucified one, but, beginning with the story of the women visiting the tomb (Luke 24:1–12), it says something more: the crucified one is also the risen one. In other words, the story continues.

> Fred B. Craddock, in *Luke*, Interpretation, lists six major theological themes that are woven through Luke 24:13–35.
> 1. Christ is known by revelation.
> 2. A summary of the gospel is recited.
> 3. The Old Testament scriptures witness to Jesus.
> 4. Christ is revealed in the sacramental meal.
> 5. Disciples understand by remembrance.
> 6. Disciples witness to what they have seen and heard.

"We had hoped . . ." (24:13–24)

The continuation of the story focuses on two disciples who are leaving Jerusalem to return to Emmaus. Although the precise location of Emmaus is difficult to determine, Luke tells us that it is located about seven miles from Jerusalem, a good walking distance in any age. As they are journeying to Emmaus, they are talking to each other and discussing everything that has happened over the past few days in Jerusalem.

These two disciples had witnessed all the events in Jerusalem—Jesus' triumphal entry upon a donkey on what we now call Palm Sunday; his trial and the way the soldiers belittled, beat, and mocked him; from a distance they had seen him hung on a cross like a common criminal; they were not able to make out his words but they saw him speaking to the criminals hanging next to him; they had seen him breathe his last breath and die; they watched him as he was laid into a tomb.

As the ancient Apostles' Creed states: He was crucified, dead, and buried. He was dead, and they were on the way from Jerusalem to Emmaus. They could not walk in silence. They had pinned their hopes on this Jesus. They had bet their lives on this one from Galilee who taught and healed with amazing grace and power. So, they could not walk without speaking; they had to share their disappointment, voice their broken dreams, put into speech their unrealized hopes. They had heard rumors about an empty tomb, but they knew—death was death. It was over. The one in whom they had invested their lives was dead.

A stranger joins them as they proceed on the road; only Luke informs his readers that this is no stranger, but the risen Lord. The two disciples on the way, however, are kept from recognizing him until the appropriate moment (Luke 24:16). As Jesus joins the disciples, he asks: "What are you discussing with each other while you walk along?" (Luke 24:17). His question stops the two disciples in their tracks—standing still and looking forlorn and sad, one of them asks: "What do you mean? Have you not heard? You must be the only one in Jerusalem who has not kept up with recent events?" "What events are those?" Jesus replies as they continue on the way from Jerusalem to Emmaus.

In response to Jesus' question, the two disciples lay out for their new visitor the gospel story—that is, they give a summary statement of the life of Christ. They say: "There was this man, Jesus of Nazareth, an amazing man, yes, even a prophet who did mighty things before God and God's people. Threatened and concerned, the chief priests and leaders handed him over to the authorities. He was condemned to death and crucified. He died, but *we had hoped* that he was the one who would redeem Israel." Although their narrative about Jesus continues, it is appropriate to break in and notice the statement "we had hoped." In this brief statement, the reaction of these disciples to the crucifixion and death of Jesus is put forth in a nutshell. Death brought discontinuity and loss of hope for these disciples and they could not imagine beyond its borders. It was an end, a cessation of all their hopes and dreams.

Yet the narrative holds hints and innuendoes that there is something more, as the two disciples tell about reports they received as they began their journey that morning. "It seems like yesterday, but all this took place three days ago. Right before we left, we got some strange news, however; some women and others had been to the tomb and came back with some preposterous news about angels, about the dead one living and the tomb being empty." With the report of the empty tomb, the disciples finish telling the gospel story. Reading in Luke's Gospel, however, we are given the impression that this story was not "gospel"—that is, "good news"—for these two disciples on the road to Emmaus. The words "we had hoped" hang in the air, as the death of Jesus appears to have canceled out his claims and calls.

"He interpreted to them the things about himself" (24:24–27)

The lack of understanding of the disciples and their shortsighted vision is also lamented by Jesus. Throughout the report of Jesus' life and death, Luke has laid the groundwork that through Jesus, God is continuing a movement, maybe one can go so far as to call it a plan of salvation. From the opening prediction of Simeon (Luke 2:34–35) through the predictions of his death (Luke 9:22, 45; 18:31) and concluding with Jesus' final word on the cross (Luke 23:46), Luke has suggested that Jesus' suffering and dying were central parts of God's redemptive move through history. As Luke tells the story, his readers probably should not be surprised that the Messiah dies. It is a necessary part of God's redemptive blueprint for human beings.

Yet the disciples on the way to Emmaus have been thrown off course by the death of Jesus. So Jesus looked at the two travelers and pondered aloud, "Was it not necessary that the Messiah should suffer these things and then enter into his glory?" (Luke 24:26). Playing on the words of men in dazzling clothes by the tomb (Luke 24:7), Jesus declares that the death of the Messiah should have been no surprise to the disciples. In order to further this claim and on a broader level the claim in Luke's Gospel that Jesus is the fulfillment of the Hebrew scriptures (see Luke 1:1–4), Jesus walked them through the Torah and the prophets, interpreting for them everything that had been written about him.

In the Jewish understanding of the scriptures, there are three major divisions within the scriptures, comparable to the stories of a building, where the lower levels support the higher, so that the higher levels are dependent on the lower ones. These are (1) the Torah, also called the five books of Moses (hence the reference to Moses in our Lukan text); this is the centerpiece and the base, consisting of Genesis–Deuteronomy; (2) the prophets, which—besides the books named for prophets like Isaiah and Hosea—include the books of Joshua, Judges, 1 and 2 Samuel, and 1 and 2 Kings (also known as the former prophets); (3) the final story, called the writings, which includes books as diverse as Esther, Psalms, and Proverbs. The image here is almost as if Jesus had scrolls of the Hebrew scriptures—which were from the two most significant layers of the tradition, the Torah and prophets—and was reading, and then interpreting to the disciples what he read. "Is it not written in Deuteronomy that the Messiah should . . . ?" "Did not Isaiah in the fifty-third chapter speak about a suffering servant . . . ?" "Have you not read in Jeremiah about . . . ?" Much of what Luke has done throughout his reporting of the gospel by tying the life of Jesus to the Old Testament scriptures, Jesus does for these wayward disciples. For early Christians the question of the relationship of Jesus to what is now called the Old Testament was probably a central question, as the authoritative word of God was contained in those scriptures and Jesus had to be understood and interpreted through that lens. In response to the skepticism of the disciples who were on the way to Emmaus, Jesus engages their scriptures and gives interpretive wisdom about a God who remains faithful to promises (recall Mary's song in Luke 1:47–55).

"He took bread, blessed and broke it . . ." (24:28–35)

Finally, the day's journey was drawing to an end and the three travelers came to a village. The disciples were tired and ready to stop and spend the night, but Jesus appeared to be going farther. They insisted, however, that he stay, that he join them for dinner, because the day was almost done. Jesus relented and stayed, and that evening they gathered at table.

At the table Jesus took bread, blessed and broke it and gave it to them. Then it was as if scales dropped from their eyes. Perhaps they looked at the hands holding the bread and recalled the feeding of five thousand with bread that was blessed, broken, and given (Luke 9:10–17). They recalled the story that the others had told them about his last meal with them and the bread blessed, broken, and given (Luke 22:19). Finally, they received revelation and recognized him. At that moment, Luke tells us, Jesus vanished and the two disciples mulled over the events of the day. They remembered the way he had touched their hearts as he had interpreted scriptures earlier in the day. The encounter with the broken bread engages the memory of the disciples, so that they put together all that has happened to them that day and realize that they have been in the presence of the risen Lord.

"Faith does not usually move from promise to fulfillment but from fulfillment to promise. Remembering is often the activating of the power of recognition" (Craddock, 283). Encountering the risen Lord puts in gear the faith of the disciples.

Slightly bewildered and slightly over-whelmed, they hurry back to Jerusalem to tell the others; they go forth to share the good news of Jesus. Upon returning to Jerusalem, they find that "the eleven" were rejoicing because Jesus had appeared to Peter. These two disciples join the chorus of witnesses and tell the others about Jesus' being made known to them in the breaking of the bread (Heb. 12:1–2). They tell the others how they had encountered him on the way to Emmaus.

> "Their witness is to other disciples, not to the world; that task must wait until they are empowered from on high. But witness and proclamation have their place among believers as well as unbelievers. The message that creates a believing community needs to be heard again and again by that community. To do so is to confirm, strengthen, encourage, and deepen faith."—Fred B. Craddock, *Luke*, Interpretation, 287–88.

On the way to Emmaus. While there are many possible reasons why this story made its way into Luke's Gospel, one might posit that it is there because all of us who claim to be followers of Jesus are like those two disciples: We are on the way. Their story on the way to Emmaus is our story on the way through our lives. Perhaps Luke tells us this story because most of us are like those two disciples. We have heard the stories of Jesus; we have heard the promises and perhaps we have experienced the joy of belief, even seen the power of faith in our lives or the lives of those close to us. We, like the disciples, have wit-nessed, if only at a distance, the life of Jesus.

At times, however, we find ourselves facing shattered dreams and broken promises along the way. We confront the craziness of our world and our lives—the pain of broken relationships, the disap-pointment of broken promises, the anguish in facing death, the sor-row of hopes that are not realized. There are times in our lives when we find that the words of the two on the way are our words. Stand-ing still, saddened, we utter: "We had hoped . . ." Like those ancient disciples, we had hoped that all our questions would be answered, all our problems solved, all our pain removed, and that we would be redeemed from all worry. At times we, like those ancient disciples, wonder if he is simply absent, unavailable—crucified, dead, and buried.

In these moments, the story from the road to Emmaus offers a possible antidote. Many have noticed that the structure of this story includes elements of early Christian worship: gospel proclamation (Luke 24:19–24), scripture reading and interpretation (Luke 24:25–27), and the Lord's Supper (Luke 24:28–35). For Christian communities throughout the centuries, the experience of those ancient disciples points to a need to worship and the bold claim that in worship the risen Lord is encountered. So, Christians gather together to worship; they gather because he has promised that where two or three are gathered there he will be also (Matt. 18:20). Christians gather to hear scripture and, like those disciples on the road to Emmaus, their hearts become strangely warmed, as John Wesley once put it. They gather, hear scripture, hear it interpreted in a sermon, and, finally, they sit at table, where bread is blessed, broken, and given to them. Luke suggests that like those disciples of old, Christians, when they participate in this way, also confront Jesus. He is made known through this word and this sacrament.

In some traditions, Communion is celebrated on the first Sunday of Advent, which is a traditional season of preparation within the Christian calendar. Of all the seasons of the church year, Advent most clearly states that we live between the times and posits a situation much like the one facing those disciples on the Emmaus road. Messiah has come. Messiah will come again. Right now, Christians find themselves on the way, preparing for his return, needing to remember that he walks with us. So as the first followers of Jesus did along the road to Emmaus, we come together, we gather, we listen, and we feast, trusting that here we meet Jesus who will walk with us along the way.

> "Finally, the Resurrection did not just teach the disciples about Jesus, or about the future. It also taught them about God. It was the supreme moment of his revelation. In particular the Resurrection could be seen as *the* great moment when God had demonstrated his power and overcome evil. It was his moment of victory."—Peter Walker, *The Weekend that Changed the World* (Louisville, Ky.: Westminster John Knox Press, 2000), 187.

Want to Know More?

About Emmaus? See Paul J. Achtemeier, *HarperCollins Bible Dictionary*, rev. ed. (San Francisco: HarperSanFrancisco, 1996), 285.

About the resurrection? See Shirley C. Guthrie, *Christian Doctrine*, rev. ed. (Louisville, Ky.: Westminster John Knox Press, 1994), 270–88.

About Jewish understandings of death and resurrection in the time of Jesus? See Werner H. Schmidt, *The Faith of the Old Testament: A History* (Philadelphia: Westminster Press, 1983), 266–77.

? Questions for Reflection

1. Why do you think the risen Christ asked "What things?" in Luke 24:19, and then waited so long to reveal himself? Did he just want to hear how the crucifixion was being interpreted by his disciples? Or was there something more he was listening for?
2. What is the significance of the moment when Christ was revealed to the two men? Compare this to Luke 22:14–20.
3. At the end of this study of Luke's Gospel, how has your understanding of the life, ministry, death, and resurrection of Jesus been changed?
4. In a few sentences, how would you summarize the basic message of Luke?

Bibliography

Bailey, Kenneth. *Poet and Peasant.* Grand Rapids: Wm. B. Eerdmans Publishing Co., 1976.

———. *Through Peasant Eyes: More Lucan Parables, Their Culture and Style.* Grand Rapids: Wm. B. Eerdmans Publishing Co., 1980.

Bonhoeffer, Dietrich. *The Cost of Discipleship.* New York: Macmillan Co., 1959.

Brown, Raymond. *The Birth of the Messiah—A Commentary on the Infancy Narratives in the Gospels of Matthew and Luke.* New York: Doubleday, 1993.

———. *The Death of the Messiah—From Gethsemane to the Grave: A Commentary on the Passion Narratives in the Four Gospels.* Vol. 2. New York: Doubleday, 1994.

Brueggemann, Walter. *Genesis.* Interpretation: A Bible Commentary for Teaching and Preaching. Louisville, Ky.: John Knox Press, 1982.

———. *The Prophetic Imagination.* Philadelphia: Fortress Press, 1978.

Calvin, John. *The Institutes of the Christian Religion.* 2 vols. Edited by John T. McNeill, translated by Ford Lewis Battles. Philadelphia: Westminster Press, 1960.

Craddock, Fred. *Luke.* Interpretation: A Bible Commentary for Teaching and Preaching. Louisville, Ky.: John Knox Press, 1990.

Fitzmyer, Joseph A. *The Gospel according to Luke I–IX: A New Translation with Introduction and Commentary.* Anchor Bible. New York: Doubleday, 1970.

Frankl, Victor. *Man's Search for Meaning: An Introduction to Logotherapy.* Translated by Ilse Lasch. Boston: Beacon Press, 1959.

Grisham, John. *The Testament.* New York: Doubleday, 1999.

Marshall, I. Howard. *Commentary on Luke.* New International Greek Testament Commentary. Grand Rapids: Wm. B. Eerdmans Publishing Co., 1978.

———. *Luke: Historian and Theologian.* Grand Rapids: Zondervan Publishing House, 1970.

Moessner, David P. *Lord of the Banquet: The Literary and Theological Significance of the Lukan Travel Narrative.* Minneapolis: Fortress Press, 1989.

Nouwen, Henri J. M. *The Return of the Prodigal Son: A Story of Homecoming.* New York: Doubleday, 1992.

O'Connor, Flannery. *The Complete Stories.* New York: Noonday Press, 1971.

Pelikan, Jaroslav Jan. *The Illustrated Jesus through the Centuries.* New Haven, Conn.: Yale University Press, 1997.

Ringe, Sharon. *Luke.* Westminster Bible Companion. Louisville, Ky.: Westminster John Knox Press, 1995.

Tannehill, Robert C. *Luke.* Abingdon New Testament Commentaries. Nashville: Abingdon Press, 1996.

Thielicke, Helmut. *The Waiting Father: Sermons on the Parables of Jesus.* Translated by John W. Doberstein. New York: Harper & Row, 1959.

Wheeler, Sondra. *Wealth as Peril and Obligation: The New Testament on Possessions.* Grand Rapids: Wm. B. Eerdmans Publishing Co., 1995.

Wuthnow, Robert. *The Crisis in the Churches: Spiritual Malaise, Fiscal Woe.* New York: Oxford University Press, 1997.

Sources of the Illustrations

Page 10: "Visit between Mary and Elizabeth," Johann David Passavant (1760–1861)

Page 18: "Baptism of Jesus," James Tissot (1836–1902)

Page 78: "Return of the Prodigal Son," Rembrandt Harmensz van Rijn (1609–69)

Page 85: "Christ on Calvary," artist unknown

Page 98: "The Supper at Emmaus," Titian (Tiziano Vecelli, 1488 or 1490–1576)

Interpretation Bible Studies
Leader's Guide

Interpretation Bible Studies (IBS), for adults and older youth, are flexible, attractive, easy-to-use, and filled with solid information about the Bible. IBS helps Christians discover the guidance and power of the scriptures for living today. Perhaps you are leading a church school class, a midweek Bible study group, or a youth group meeting, or simply using this in your own personal study. Whatever the setting may be, we hope you find this *Leader's Guide* helpful. Since every context and group is different, this *Leader's Guide* does not presume to tell you how to structure Bible study for your situation. Instead, the *Leader's Guide* seeks to offer choices—a number of helpful suggestions for leading a successful Bible study using IBS.

> "The church that no longer hears the essential message of the Scriptures soon ceases to understand what it is for and is open to be captured by the dominant religious philosophy of the moment."— James D. Smart, *The Strange Silence of the Bible in the Church: A Study in Hermeneutics* (Philadelphia: Westminster Press, 1970), 10.

How Should I Teach IBS?

1. Explore the Format

There is a wealth of information in IBS, perhaps more than you can use in one session. In this case, more is better. IBS has been designed to give you a well-stocked buffet of content and teachable insights. Pick and choose what suits your group's needs. Perhaps you will want to split units into two or more sessions, or combine units into a single session. Perhaps you will decide to use only a portion of a unit and then move on to the next unit. *There is not a structured theme or teaching focus to each unit that must be followed for IBS to be used.* Rather, IBS offers the flexibility to adjust to whatever suits your context.

"The more we bring to the Bible, the more we get from the Bible." —William Barclay, *A Beginner's Guide to the New Testament* (Louisville, Ky.: Westminster John Knox Press, 1995), vii.

A recent survey of both professional and volunteer church educators revealed that their number one concern was that Bible study materials be teacher-friendly. IBS is indeed teacher-friendly in two important ways. First, since IBS provides abundant content and a flexible design, teachers can shape the lessons creatively, responding to the needs of the group and employing a wide variety of teaching methods. Second, those who wish more specific suggestions for planning the sessions can find them at the Geneva Press web site on the Internet (**www.ppcpub.org**). Click the "IBS Teacher Helps" button to access teaching suggestions for each IBS unit as well as helpful quotations, selections from Bible dictionaries and encyclopedias, and other teaching helps.

IBS is not only teacher-friendly, it is also discussion-friendly. Given the opportunity, most adults and young people relish the chance to talk about the kind of issues raised in IBS. The secret, then, is to determine what works with your group, what will get them to talk. Several good methods for stimulating discussion are presented in this *Leader's Guide,* and once you learn your group, you can apply one of these methods and get the group discussing the Bible and its relevance in their lives.

The format of every IBS unit consists of several features:

a. Body of the Unit. This is the main content, consisting of interesting and informative commentary on the passage and scholarly insight into the biblical text and its significance for Christians today.

b. Sidebars. These are boxes that appear scattered throughout the body of the unit, with maps, photos, quotations, and intriguing ideas. Some sidebars can be identified quickly by a symbol, or icon, that helps the reader know what type of information can be found in that sidebar. There are icons for illustrations, key terms, pertinent quotes, and more.

c. Want to Know More? Each unit includes a "Want to Know More?" section that guides learners who wish to dig deeper and consult other resources. If your church library does not have the resources mentioned, you can look up the information in other standard Bible dictionaries, encyclopedias, and handbooks, or you can find much of this information at the Geneva Press Web site (see last page of this Guide).

d. Questions for Reflection. The unit ends with questions to help the learners think more deeply about the biblical passage and its pertinence for today. These questions are provided as examples only, and teachers are encouraged both to develop their own list of questions and to gather questions from the group. These discussion questions do not usually have specific "correct" answers. Again, the flexibility of IBS allows you to use these questions at the end of the group time, at the beginning, interspersed throughout, or not at all.

> "The trick is to make the Bible our book."—Duncan S. Ferguson, *Bible Basics: Mastering the Content of the Bible* (Louisville, Ky.: Westminster John Knox Press, 1995), 3.

2. Select a Teaching Method

Here are ten suggestions. The format of IBS allows you to choose what direction you will take as you plan to teach. Only you will know how your lesson should best be designed for your group. Some adult groups prefer the lecture method, while others prefer a high level of free-ranging discussion. Many youth groups like interaction, activity, the use of music, and the chance to talk about their own experiences and feelings. Here is a list of a few possible approaches. Let your own creativity add to the list!

a. Let's Talk about What We've Learned. In this approach, all group members are requested to read the scripture passage and the IBS unit before the group meets. Ask the group members to make notes about the main issues, concerns, and questions they see in the passage. When the group meets, these notes are collected, shared, and discussed. This method depends, of course, on the group's willingness to do some "homework."

b. What Do We Want and Need to Know? This approach begins by having the whole group read the scripture passage together. Then, drawing from your study of the IBS, you, as the teacher, write on a board or flip chart two lists:

(1) Things we should know to better understand this passage (content information related to the passage, for example, historical insights about political contexts, geographical landmarks, economic nuances, etc.), and

(2) Four or five "important issues we should talk about regarding this passage" (with implications for today—how the issues in the biblical context continue into today, for example, issues of idolatry or fear).

> "Although small groups can meet for many purposes and draw upon many different resources, the one resource which has shaped the life of the Church more than any other throughout its long history has been the Bible." —Roberta Hestenes, *Using the Bible in Groups* (Philadelphia: Westminster Press, 1983), 14.

Allow the group to add to either list, if they wish, and use the lists to lead into a time of learning, reflection, and discussion. This approach is suitable for those settings where there is little or no advanced preparation by the students.

c. Hunting and Gathering. Start the unit by having the group read the scripture passage together. Then divide the group into smaller clusters (perhaps having as few as one person), each with a different assignment. Some clusters can discuss one or more of the "Questions for Reflection." Others can look up key terms or people in a Bible dictionary or track down other biblical references found in the body of the unit. After the small clusters have had time to complete their tasks, gather the entire group again and lead them through the study material, allowing each cluster to contribute what it learned.

d. From Question Mark to Exclamation Point. This approach begins with contemporary questions and then moves to the biblical content as a response to those questions. One way to do this is for you to ask the group, at the beginning of the class, a rephrased version of one or more of the "Questions for Reflection" at the end of the study unit. For example, one of the questions at the end of the unit on Exodus 3:1–4:17 in the IBS *Exodus* volume reads,

> Moses raised four protests, or objections, to God's call. Contemporary people also raise objections to God's call. In what ways are these similar to Moses' protests? In what ways are they different?

This question assumes familiarity with the biblical passage about Moses, so the question would not work well before the group has explored the passage. However, try rephrasing this question as an opening exercise; for example:

Here is a thought experiment: Let's assume that God, who called people in the Bible to do daring and risky things, still calls people today to tasks of faith and courage. In the Bible, God called Moses from a burning bush and called Isaiah in a moment of ecstatic worship in the Temple. How do you think God's call is experienced by people today? Where do you see evidence of people saying "yes" to God's call? When people say "no" or raise an objection to God's call, what reasons do they give (to themselves, to God)?

Posing this or a similar question at the beginning will generate discussion and raise important issues, and then it can lead the group into an exploration of the biblical passage as a resource for thinking even more deeply about these questions.

e. Let's Go to the Library. From your church library, your pastor's library, or other sources, gather several good commentaries on the book of the Bible you are studying. Among the trustworthy commentaries are those in the Interpretation series (John Knox Press) and the Westminster Bible Companion series (Westminster John Knox Press). Divide your group into smaller clusters and give one commentary to each cluster (one or more of the clusters can be given the IBS volume instead of a full-length commentary). Ask each cluster to read the biblical passage you are studying and then to read the section of the commentary that covers that passage (if your group is large, you may want to make photocopies of the commentary material with proper permission, of course). The task of each cluster is to name the two or three most important insights they discover about the biblical passage by reading and talking together about the commentary material. When you reassemble the larger group to share these insights, your group will gain not only a variety of insights about the passage but also a sense that differing views of the same text are par for the course in biblical interpretation.

f. Working Creatively Together. Begin with a creative group task, tied to the main thrust of the study. For example, if the study is on the Ten Commandments, a parable, or a psalm, have the group rewrite the Ten Commandments, the parable, or the psalm in contemporary language. If the passage is an epistle, have the group write a letter to their own congregation. Or if the study is a narrative, have the group role-play the characters in the story or write a page describing the story from the point of view of one of the characters. After completion of the task, read and discuss the biblical passage, asking for interpretations and applications from the group and tying in IBS material as it fits the flow of the discussion.

g. Singing Our Faith. Begin the session by singing (or reading) together a hymn that alludes to the biblical passage being studied (or to the theological themes in the passage). Most hymnals have an index of scriptural allusions. For example, if you are studying the unit from the IBS volume on Psalm 121, you can sing "I to the Hills Will Lift My Eyes," "Sing Praise to God, Who Reigns Above," or another hymn based on Psalm 121. Let the group reflect on the thoughts and feelings evoked by the hymn, then move to the biblical passage, allowing the biblical text and the IBS material to underscore, clarify, refine, and deepen the discussion stimulated by the hymn. If you are ambitious, you may ask the group to write a new hymn at the end of the study! (Many hymnals have indexes in the back or companion volumes that help the user match hymns to scripture passages or topics.)

h. Fill in the Blanks. In order to help the learners focus on the content of the biblical passage, at the beginning of the session ask each member of the group to read the biblical passage and fill out a brief questionnaire about the details of the passage (provide a copy for each learner or write the questions on the board). For example, if you are studying the unit in the IBS *Matthew* volume on Matthew 22:1–14, the questionnaire could include questions such as the following:

—In this story, Jesus compares the kingdom of heaven to what?
—List the various responses of those who were invited to the king's banquet but who did not come.
—When his invitation was rejected, how did the king feel? What did the king do?
—In the second part of the story, when the king saw a man at the banquet without a wedding garment, what did the king say? What did the man say? What did the king do?
—What is the saying found at the end of this story?

Gather the group's responses to the questions and perhaps encourage discussion. Then lead the group through the IBS material helping the learners to understand the meanings of these details and the significance of the passage for today. Feeling creative? Instead of a fill-in-the blanks questionnaire, create a crossword puzzle from names and words in the biblical passage.

i. Get the Picture. In this approach, stimulate group discussion by incorporating a painting, photograph, or other visual object into the lesson. You can begin by having the group examine and comment on this visual or you can introduce the visual later in the lesson—it depends on the object used. If, for example, you are studying the unit Exodus 3:1–4:17 in the IBS *Exodus* volume, you may want to view Paul Koli's very colorful painting *The Burning Bush.* Two sources for this painting are *The Bible Through Asian Eyes,* edited by Masao Takenaka and Ron O'Grady (National City, Calif.: Pace Publishing Co., 1991), and *Imaging the Word: An Arts and Lectionary Resource,* vol. 3, edited by Susan A. Blain (Cleveland: United Church Press, 1996).

j. Now Hear This. Especially if your class is large, you may want to use the lecture method. As the teacher, you prepare a presentation on the biblical passage, using as many resources as you have available plus your own experience, but following the content of the IBS unit as a guide. You can make the lecture even more lively by asking the learners at various points along the way to refer to the visuals and quotes found in the "sidebars." A place can be made for questions (like the ones at the end of the unit)—either at the close of the lecture or at strategic points along the way.

> "It is . . . important to call a Bible study group back to what the text being discussed actually says, especially when an individual has gotten off on some tangent." —Richard Robert Osmer, *Teaching for Faith: A Guide for Teachers of Adult Classes* (Louisville, Ky.: Westminster John Knox Press, 1992), 71.

3. Keep These Teaching Tips in Mind

There are no surefire guarantees for a teaching success. However, the following suggestions can increase the chances for a successful study:

a. Always Know Where the Group Is Headed. Take ample time beforehand to prepare the material. Know the main points of the study, and know the destination. Be flexible, and encourage discussion, but don't lose sight of where you are headed.

b. Ask Good Questions; Don't Be Afraid of Silence. Ideally, a discussion blossoms spontaneously from the reading of the scripture. But more often than not, a discussion must be drawn from the group members by a series of well-chosen questions. After asking each question, give the group members time to answer. Let them think, and don't be threatened by a season of silence. Don't feel that every question must have an answer, and that as leader, you must supply every answer. Facilitate discussion by getting the group members to cooperate with each other. Sometimes, the original question can be restated. Sometimes it is helpful to ask a follow-up question like "What makes this a hard question to answer?"

Ask questions that encourage explanatory answers. Try to avoid questions that can be answered simply "Yes" or "No." Rather than asking, "Do you think Moses was frightened by the burning bush?" ask, "What do you think Moses was feeling and experiencing as he stood before the burning bush?" If group members answer with just one word, ask a follow-up question like "Why do you think this is so?" Ask questions about their feelings and opinions, mixed within questions about facts or details. Repeat their responses or restate their response to reinforce their contributions to the group.

> "Studies of learning reveal that while people remember approximately 10% of what they hear, they remember up to 90% of what they say. Therefore, to increase the amount of learning that occurs, increase the amount of talking about the Bible which each member does."—Roberta Hestenes, *Using the Bible in Groups* (Philadelphia: Westminster Press, 1983), 17.

Most studies can generate discussion by asking open-ended questions. Depending on the group, several types of questions can work. Some groups will respond well to content questions that can be answered from reading the IBS comments or the biblical passage. Others will respond well to questions about feelings or thoughts. Still others will respond to questions that challenge them to new thoughts or that may not have exact answers. Be sensitive to the group's dynamic in choosing questions.

Some suggested questions are: What is the point of the passage? Who are the main characters? Where is the tension in the story? Why does it say (this)_____, and not (that) _____? What raises questions for you? What terms need defining? What are the new ideas? What doesn't make sense? What bothers or troubles you about this passage? What keeps you from living the truth of this passage?

c. Don't Settle for the Ordinary. There is nothing like a surprise. Think of special or unique ways to present the ideas of the study. Upset the applecart of the ordinary. Even though the passage may be familiar, look for ways to introduce suspense. Remember that a little mystery can capture the imagination. Change your routine.

Along with the element of surprise, humor can open up a discussion. Don't be afraid to laugh. A well-chosen joke or cartoon may present the central theme in a way that a lecture would have stymied.

Sometimes a passage is too familiar. No one speaks up because everyone feels that all that could be said has been said. Choose an unfamiliar translation from which to read, or if the passage is from a Gospel, compare the story across two or more Gospels and note differences. It is amazing what insights can be drawn from seeing something strange in what was thought to be familiar.

d. Feel Free to Supplement the IBS Resources with Other Material. Consult other commentaries or resources. Tie in current events with the lesson. Scour newspapers or magazines for stories that touch on the issues of the study. Sometimes the lyrics of a song, or a section of prose from a well-written novel will be just the right seasoning for the study.

e. And Don't Forget to Check the Web. Check out our site on the World Wide Web (www.ppcpub.org). Click the "IBS Teacher Helps" button to access teaching suggestions. Several possibilities for applying the teaching methods suggested above for individual IBS units will be available. Feel free to download this material.

> "The Bible is literature, but it is much more than literature. It is the holy book of Jews and Christians, who find there a manifestation of God's presence." —Kathleen Norris, *The Psalms* (New York: Riverhead Books, 1997), xxii.

f. Stay Close to the Biblical Text. Don't forget that the goal is to learn the Bible. Return to the text again and again. Avoid making the mistake of reading the passage only at the beginning of the study, and then wandering away to comments on top of comments from that point on. Trust in the power and presence of the Holy Spirit to use the truths of the passage to work within the lives of the study participants.

What If I Am Using IBS in Personal Bible Study?

If you are using IBS in your personal Bible study, you can experiment and explore a variety of ways. You may choose to read straight through the study without giving any attention to the sidebars or other features. Or you may find yourself interested in a question or unfamiliar with a key term, and you can allow the sidebars "Want to Know More?" and "Questions for Reflection" to lead you into deeper learning on these issues. Perhaps you will want to have a few commentaries or a Bible dictionary available to pursue what interests you. As was suggested in one of the teaching methods above, you may want to begin with the questions at the end, and then read the Bible passage followed by the IBS material. Trust the IBS resources to provide good and helpful information, and then follow your interests!

Want to Know More?

About leading Bible study groups? See Roberta Hestenes, *Using the Bible in Groups* (Philadelphia: Westminster Press, 1983).

About basic Bible content? See Duncan S. Ferguson, *Bible Basics: Mastering the Content of the Bible* (Louisville, Ky.: Westminster John Knox Press, 1995); William M. Ramsay, *The Westminster Guide to the Books of the Bible* (Louisville, Ky.: Westminster John Knox Press, 1994).

About the development of the Bible? See John Barton, *How the Bible Came to Be* (Louisville, Ky.: Westminster John Knox Press, 1997).

About the meaning of difficult terms? See Donald K. McKim, *Westminster Dictionary of Theological Terms* (Louisville, Ky.: Westminster John Knox Press, 1996); Paul J. Achtemeier, *Harper's Bible Dictionary* (San Francisco: Harper & Row, 1985).

For more information about IBS,
click the "IBS Teacher Helps" button at
www.ppcpub.org